GW00750651

Cambridge English

PROFICIENCY

CERTIFICATE OF PROFICIENCY IN ENGLISH

WITH ANSWERS

2

AUTHENTIC EXAMINATION PAPERS
FROM CAMBRIDGE ENGLISH
LANGUAGE ASSESSMENT

Cambridge University Press
www.cambridge.org/elt

Cambridge Assessment English
www.cambridgeenglish.org

Information on this title: www.cambridge.org/9781107686939

© Cambridge University Press and UCLES 2015

First published 2015

20 19 18 17 16 15 14 13 12 11 10 9 8 7 6 5

Printed in Malaysia by Vivar Printing

A catalogue record for this publication is available from the British Library

ISBN 978-1-107-68693-9 Student's Book with answers
ISBN 978-1-107-63792-4 Student's Book without answers
ISBN 978-1-107-64651-3 Student's Book with answers with audio
ISBN 978-1-107-64764-0 Audio CDs (2)

Contents

Thanks and acknowledgements   *4*

Introduction   *5*

Test 1 Reading and Use of English   *8*
Writing   *20*
Listening   *22*
Speaking   *27*

Test 2 Reading and Use of English   *28*
Writing   *40*
Listening   *42*
Speaking   *47*

Test 3 Reading and Use of English   *48*
Writing   *60*
Listening   *62*
Speaking   *67*

Test 4 Reading and Use of English   *68*
Writing   *80*
Listening   *82*
Speaking   *87*

Test 1 Speaking test frames   *88*
Test 2 Speaking test frames   *92*
Test 3 Speaking test frames   *96*
Test 4 Speaking test frames   *100*

Marks and results   *104*

Test 1 Key and transcript   *126*
Test 2 Key and transcript   *135*
Test 3 Key and transcript   *144*
Test 4 Key and transcript   *152*

Sample answer sheets   *160*

Visual materials for the Speaking test   *colour section at the back of the book*

Thanks and acknowledgements

The authors and publishers acknowledge the following sources of copyright material and are grateful for the permissions granted. While every effort has been made, it has not always been possible to identify the sources of all the material used, or to trace all copyright holders. If any omissions are brought to our notice, we will be happy to include the appropriate acknowledgements on reprinting.

Text acknowledgements

New Scientist for the simplified extract on p. 10 'Mission to Mars', *New Scientist* 09/03/2013; for the re-written extract on p. 64 'The psychology of colour: Why winners wear red' by Daniel Elkan, *New Scientist* 28/08/2009; for the re-written extract on p. 68 'Stop the Rot' by James Mitchel Crow, *New Scientist* 19/06/2010; Guardian News and Media for the simplified extract on p. 14 'Blogging: the fine art of the confessional' by Scott Rosenberg, *The Guardian* 13/03/2011, for the simplified extract on p. 16 'Build it yourself at the UK's first bamboo bike workshop' by James Stewart, *The Guardian* 16/11/2012, for the adapted extract on p. 28 'A Life of their own' by Katharine Whitehorn, *The Observer* 30/09/2014, for the adapted extract on p. 39 'Forty years on, why we're still living in the moon's shadow' by Christopher Riley, *The Guardian* 22/12/2012, for the adapted extract on p. 45 'Here's a fresh slant on suburbia' by R. Moore, *Observer New Review* 24/02/2013, for the adapted extract on p. 51 'Without books, we would be very different people' by Gail Rebuck, *The Guardian* 31/12/2011, for the adapted extract on p. 59(A) 'Old music: Robert Wyatt – At Last I Am Free' by George Chesterton, *The Guardian* 10/01/2013, for the adapted extract on p. 59(B) 'Old music: Roy Harper – Another Day' by George Chesterton, *The Guardian* 28/06/2012, for the adapted extract on p. 59(C) 'Old music: Soft Cell – Say Hello Wave Goodbye' by Nick Hopkins, *The Guardian* 28/02/2013, for the adapted extract on p. 59(D) 'Old music: Rod Stewart – Maggie May' by Greg Freeman, *The Guardian* 18/10/2012, for the adapted extract on p. 59(E) 'Old music: Tom Waits – Martha' by Jon Lloyd, *The Guardian* 30/05/2012, for the adapted extract on p. 62 'Up Front, Prickly About Hedgehogs' by K Whitehorn, *The Guardian* 10/02/2013, for the simplified extract on p. 71 'How do we find time for what matters in the digital age?' by Tom Chatfield, *The Guardian* 26/01/2012, for the simplified extract on p. 76 'London Zoo's new Tiger Territory: built for the animals first, and visitors second?' by Oliver Wainwright, *The Guardian* 20/03/2013; Thomson Reuters for the simplified extract on p. 19 from 'How to study law' Bradney et al, *Sweet & Maxwell*, 1991. Reprinted with permission; National Public Radio, Inc for the simplified extract on p. 22 © 2013 National Public Radio, Inc. New Report titled "Monkey Calls Could Offer Clues For Origin Of Human Speech" was originally broadcast on NPR's All Things Considered on April 9, 2013, and is used with the permission of NPR. Any unauthorized duplication is strictly prohibited; Adapted extract on p. 23 from 'News Of The World: Kate Adie Interviewed On Music And War' by W Wallace, *The Quietus*, 07/03/2011. From News Of The World: Kate Adie Interviewed On Music And War by W Wallace with permission of Wyndham Wallace and Kate Adie Chief Correspondent, BBC News and author of Fighting on the Home Front: The Legacy of Women in World War 1. Hodder & Stoughton, 2013; ABC Radio National for the adapted extract on p. 25 from 'Remembering together' presented by Lynne Malcolm 27/05/2012. With permission; *The Independent* for the adapted extract on p. 31 'Journey to the Antarctic Ocean' by Charlie Cooper, The Independent 26/09/12, for the adapted extract on p. 34 'Are you an Oscar or an Elmo' by Emily Jupp, *The Independent* 31/07/12, for the adapted extract on p. 54 'Manet and woman: Portraying life' by Adrian Hamilton, *The Independent* 22/01/13; Random House Group and Bill Bryson for the adapted extract on p. 36 from *Down Under* by Bill Bryson, *Black Swan*, 2010. Copyright © Bill Bryson, 2010. Reprinted with permission; Adapted extract on p. 42 from 'Elon Musk on Team Building, Warren Buffet and Mars' 09/02/2013. An evening with Elon Musk and Alison van Diggelen, 2013-01-22, CHM Lecture Collection, Lot X6753.2013, Digital Archive, Catalog Number 102746849, Computer History Museum with permission; CBA for the adapted extract on p. 42 from 'Viktor Mayer-Schönberger on forgetting in a digital age' 22/09/2009. *Spark* with Nora Young. Reprinted with permission; Rewritten extract on p. 44 from 'Feral animals in Australia', www.environment.gov.au/biodiversity/invasive/ferals/index.htm, licenced under a Creative Commons Attribution 3.0 Australia licence © Commonwealth of Australia 2013; Lonely Planet for the simplified extract on p. 56 'Lake Malawi's lost resort' by Marina Lewycka. Adapted with permission from Better than Fiction © 2012 Lonely Planet; Patrick Schwerdtfeger for the adapted extract on p. 62 from 'Go BIG!'. Reprinted with permission; The Sunday Times for the simplified extract on p. 74 'Kapow! It's Proust' by Robert Collins *The Sunday Times* 02/12/2012; The Open University and John Wiley & Sons for the adapted extract on p. 79 from 'Understanding Childhood' by Woodhead & Montgomery (eds), *The Open University/John Wiley & Sons*. Reprinted with permission; Teapigs for the rewritten extract on p. 82 'Teapigs – Clever Marketing By Tetley Tea' *Axel and Sophie Steenbergs Blog*. Post 06/2010 by Nick Kilby, Co-founder of Teapigs, with permission from www.teapigs.co.uk; ABC for the rewritten extract on p. 82 from a transcript of 'Cardboard, paper and play' presented by Antony Funnell. Reproduced by permission of the Australian Broadcasting Corporation (c) 2012 ABC. All rights reserved.

Photo acknowledgements

Test 1 Photo 1A C2: © Aurora Photos/Alamy; Test 1 Photo 1B C2: © Chris Linder/Visuals Unlimited/Corbis; Test 1 Photo 1C C2: © Sutton Images/Corbis; Test 2 Photo 2A C3: © Redlink/Corbis; Test 2 Photo 2B C3: © © Moodboard/Corbis; Test 2 Photo 2C C3: © Atlantide Phototravel/Corbis; Test 3 Photo 3A C4: © Jon Feingersh Photography Inc./Blend Images/Corbis; Test 3 Photo 3B C4: © Helen King/Corbis ; Test 3 Photo 3C C4: © Phil Boorman/cultura/Corbis; Test 3 Photo 3D C4: © Helen King/Corbis ; Test 4 Photo 4A C5: © Chad Ehlers/Alamy; Test 4 Photo 4B C5: © Atlantide Phototravel/Corbis.

The recordings which accompany this book were made at dsound, London.

Introduction

This collection of four complete practice tests comprises papers from the Cambridge English: Proficiency (CPE) examination; students can practise with these tests on their own or with the help of a teacher.

The CPE examination is part of a suite of general English examinations produced by Cambridge English Language Assessment. This suite consists of five examinations that have similar characteristics but are designed for different levels of English language ability. Within the five levels, CPE is at Level C2 in the Council of Europe's *Common European Framework of Reference for Languages: Learning, teaching, assessment.* It has been accredited by Ofqual, the statutory regulatory authority in England, at Level 3 in the National Qualifications Framework. CPE is recognised by universities, employers, governments and other organisations around the world as proof of the ability to use English to function at the highest levels of academic and professional life.

Examination	Council of Europe Framework Level	UK National Qualifications Framework Level
Cambridge English: Proficiency *Certificate of Proficiency in English (CPE)*	C2	3
Cambridge English: Advanced *Certificate in Advanced English (CAE)*	C1	2
Cambridge English: First *First Certificate in English (FCE)*	B2	1
Cambridge English: Preliminary *Preliminary English Test (PET)*	B1	Entry 3
Cambridge English: Key *Key English Test (KET)*	A2	Entry 2

Further information

The information contained in this practice book is designed to be an overview of the exam. For a full description of all of the above exams including information about task types, testing focus and preparation, please see the relevant handbooks which can be obtained from Cambridge English Language Assessment at the address below or from the website at: www.cambridgeenglish.org

Cambridge English Language Assessment
1 Hills Road
Cambridge CB1 2EU
United Kingdom

Telephone: +44 1223 553997
Fax: +44 1223 553621
e-mail: helpdesk@cambridgeenglish.org

The structure of CPE: an overview

The CPE examination consists of four papers:

Reading and Use of English 1 hour 30 minutes
This paper consists of seven parts with 53 questions. For Parts 1 to 4, the test contains texts with accompanying grammar and vocabulary tasks, and discrete items with a grammar and vocabulary focus. For Parts 5 to 7, the test contains texts and accompanying reading comprehension tasks.

Writing 1 hour 30 minutes
This paper consists of two parts which carry equal marks. In Part 1, which is compulsory, candidates must write an essay with a discursive focus of between 240 and 280 words. The task requires candidates to summarise and evaluate the key ideas contained in two texts of approximately 100 words each.

In Part 2, there are five questions from which candidates must choose one to write about. The range of tasks from which questions may be drawn includes an article, a letter, a report, a review, and an essay (set text questions only). The last question (Question 5) is based on the set texts. These set texts remain on the list for two years. Look on the website, or contact the Cambridge English Language Assessment Centre Exams Manager in your area for the up-to-date list of set texts. Question 5 has two options from which candidates choose one to write about. In this part, candidates write between 280 and 320 words.

Assessment is based on the Assessment Scales, comprising four subscales: Content, Communicative Achievement, Organisation, and Language.

Listening 40 minutes (approximately)
This paper consists of four parts with 30 questions. Each part contains a recorded text or texts and corresponding comprehension tasks. Each part is heard twice.

Speaking 16 minutes
The Speaking test consists of three parts. The standard test format is two candidates and two examiners. One examiner acts as interlocutor and manages the interaction either by asking questions or providing cues for the candidates. The other acts as assessor and does not join in the conversation. The test consists of short exchanges with the interlocutor, a collaborative task involving both candidates and an individual long turn followed by a three-way discussion.

Grading
The overall CPE grade is based on the total score gained in all four papers. All candidates receive a Statement of Results which includes a graphical profile of their performance in all four skills and Use of English. Certificates are given

to candidates who pass the examination with grade A, B or C. Candidates whose performance is below C2 level, but falls within Level C1, receive a Cambridge English certificate stating they have demonstrated ability at C1 level. Candidates whose performance falls below Level C1 do not receive a certificate.

For further information on grading and results, go to the Cambridge English Language Assessment website (see page 5).

Test 1

READING AND USE OF ENGLISH (1 hour 30 minutes)

Part 1

For questions **1–8**, read the text below and decide which answer (**A, B, C** or **D**) best fits each gap.

Mark your answers **on the separate answer sheet**.

There is an example at the beginning (**0**).

0	**A** disagreement	**B** dissent	**C** dispute	**D** discord

0	A	B	C	D
	▭	▭	▬	▭

England's breakfast revolution

The importance of a good breakfast is beyond **(0)** .... according to health experts, but in historical terms breakfast is a relatively new arrival in England, with descriptions of breakfast seldom **(1)** .... in medieval literature. **(2)** ...., there are scattered references to travellers having a meal at dawn before **(3)** .... on arduous journeys, and to the sick sitting down to breakfast for medicinal reasons, but most people went without unless they were monarchs or nobles.

However, in the sixteenth century it gradually became the **(4)** ...., not the exception. Some writers have **(5)** .... this to the greater availability of food. Proponents of this view have not always considered other profound social changes. For example, new **(6)** .... of employment may well offer a plausible explanation for the greater importance now **(7)** .... to breakfast, as individuals were increasingly employed for a prescribed number of hours. Often this involved starting work extremely early. Thus, having a meal first thing in the morning was **(8)** .... in necessity, and was no longer associated with social status alone.

1 **A** displaying   **B** manifesting   **C** disclosing   **D** featuring

2 **A** Deservedly   **B** Admittedly   **C** Conceivably   **D** Assuredly

3 **A** engaging   **B** launching   **C** embarking   **D** committing

4 **A** norm   **B** prototype   **C** standard   **D** trait

5 **A** attributed   **B** assigned   **C** accounted   **D** accorded

6 **A** figures   **B** shapes   **C** lines   **D** patterns

7 **A** linked   **B** fixed   **C** attached   **D** secured

8 **A** embedded   **B** rooted   **C** entrenched   **D** founded

Part 2

For questions **9–16**, read the text below and think of the word which best fits each space. Use only **one** word in each space. There is an example at the beginning (**0**). Write your answers **IN CAPITAL LETTERS on the separate answer sheet.**

Example: | **0** | F | O | R | | | | | | | | | | | | | | | |

Mission to Mars

Wanted: a middle-aged, married couple **(0)** .... a 501-day round trip to Mars. Applicants must be physically and emotionally robust.

This will be the profile of the very first Martian astronauts if multi-millionaire Dennis Tito's plans to launch a capsule on 5 January 2018 actually **(9)** .... to fruition. The capsule will take the crew to about 160 km above Mars. The spacecraft will use the gravity of Mars to allow it to return to Earth without burning any more fuel, for fuel efficiency is a priority – the 2018 deadline has been fixed **(10)** .... the next launch window when Mars and Earth align again isn't **(11)** .... 2031. It's a **(12)** .... order, but the race is on to develop systems involving totally new technologies. **(13)** .... that these can be put in place soon enough, the spacecraft might just **(14)** .... it. But even if it **(15)** .... leaves Earth, the efforts to achieve these ambitious goals will not be in **(16)** ...., as they will lead to valuable advances for future missions.

Part 3

For questions **17–24**, read the text below. Use the word given in capitals at the end of some of the lines to form a word that fits in the space in the same line. There is an example at the beginning (**0**). tWrite your answers **IN CAPITAL LETTERS on the separate answer sheet**.

Example: **0** T E N D E N C Y

CRYING

Charles Darwin thought that the human **(0)** .... to cry had no obvious **TEND**

(17) .... purpose. He was almost certainly wrong. More recently scientists have **EVOLVE**

pointed to its social **(18)** ...., with psychiatrist John Bowlby highlighting the role **SIGN**

of crying in developing the **(19)** .... between mother and child. Many believe **ATTACH**

that tears, at least during childhood, are mainly an expression of **(20)** .... **HELP**

However, the persistence of crying into adulthood is harder to explain. It seems

that the sound of crying becomes considerably less important than the visual

signal it conveys. It may have been **(21)** .... to early human communities as a **ADVANTAGE**

means of promoting trust and social connectedness.

Tears can undoubtedly have other causes too. We may cry to express sympathy

for those suffering terrible **(22)** .... Furthermore, tears can be shed **JUST**

(23) ...., rather to our embarrassment, when we hear inspiring music or moving **VOLUNTARY**

speeches. We may cry when watching a sentimental film, but interestingly, this is

more likely to occur in company than when we are alone. The social function of

crying would seem to be **(24)** ...., but research continues. **DENY**

Part 4

For questions **25–30**, complete the second sentence so that it has a similar meaning to the first sentence, using the word given. **Do not change the word given.** You must use between **three** and **eight** words, including the word given. Here is an example (**0**).

Example:

0 Do you mind if I watch you while you paint?

objection

Do you .... you while you paint?

0	*have any objection to my watching*

Write **only** the missing words **on the separate answer sheet**.

---

25 I hope the committee will consider this new information when they meet next week.

account

I hope this new information .... when the

committee meet next week.

26 James did not find it difficult to answer the interviewer's questions.

coming

James had no .... the interviewer's questions.

27 The more experienced members of the expedition were made responsible for finding food.

charge

The more experienced members of the expedition ....

finding food.

28 The agent said he no longer thought that Sam Bowker would ever appear in a Hollywood film.

hope

The agent said he .... appearing in a Hollywood film.

29 My father said that the portrait did not look like him.

resemblance

My father said that the portrait .... him.

30 Leo doesn't understand why his sister is opposing his plan.

what

Leo doesn't understand .... his plan is.

Part 5

You are going to read an article about the history of blogging. For questions **31–36**, choose the answer (**A**, **B**, **C** or **D**) which you think fits best according to the text. Mark your answers **on the separate answer sheet**.

Blogging: Confessing to the world

Some time ago, a website highlighted the risks of public check-ins – online announcements of your where-abouts. The site's point was blunt: you may think you are just telling the world, 'Hey, I'm at this place' – but you are also advertising your out-and-about-ness to all kinds of people everywhere – not all of them people you might like to bump into. This appeared to confirm the growing awareness that there might be a downside to all the frantic sharing the web has enabled. The vast new opportunities to publish any and every aspect of our lives to a potentially global audience hold out all sorts of tantalising possibilities: Wealth! Fame! So we plunge into the maelstrom of the internet, tossing confessions, personal photos and stories into the digital vortex. Too late we realise that the water is crowded and treacherous – and we are lost.

Depressing? Perhaps, but don't give up. This future has a map, drawn for us years ago by a reckless group of online pioneers. In the early days of the web, they sailed these waters and located all the treacherous shoals. They got fired from their jobs, found and lost friends and navigated celebrity's temptations and perils – all long before the invention of social networking. These pioneers, the first wave of what we now call bloggers, have already been where the rest of us seem to be going. Before their tales scroll off our collective screen, it's worth spending a little time with them. After all, those who cannot learn from history are doomed to repost it.

In January 1994, Justin Hall, a 19-year-old student, began posting to the 'WWW', as it was then known, something inhabited mostly by grad students, scientists and a handful of precocious teens like him. The web had been invented at CERN, the international physics lab in Switzerland, so researchers could more easily share their work. Hall saw something else: an opportunity to share his life. Link by link, he built a hypertext edifice of autobiography, a dense thicket of verbal self-exposure leavened with photos and art. In January 1996, on a dare, he began posting a daily blog, and readers flocked to the spectacle of a reckless young man pushing the boundaries of this new medium in every direction at once.

Hall's ethos was absolute: cross his path and you could appear on his site; no topic was taboo. Certainly, this was the work of an exhibitionist, but there was also a rigour and beauty to his project that only a snob would refuse to call art. One day though, visitors to Hall's site discovered his home page gone, replaced with a single anguished video titled *Dark Night*. His story tumbled out; he'd fallen spectacularly in love, but when he started writing about it on his site he was told 'either the blog goes, or I do'. He'd published his life on the internet and, Hall protested, 'it makes people not trust me'. The blog went, but the dilemma persists. Sharing online is great. But if you expect your song of yourself to 'make people want to be with you', you'll be disappointed.

In 2002, Heather Armstrong, a young web worker in Los Angeles, had a blog called Dooce. Occasionally, she wrote about her job at a software company. One day an anonymous colleague sent the address of Armstrong's blog to every vice president at her company – including some whom she'd mocked – and that was the end of her job. Those who study the peculiar social patterns of the networked world have a term to describe what was at work here. They call it the 'online distribution effect': that feeling so many of us have that we can get away with saying things online that we'd never dream of saying in person. But our digital lives are interwoven with our real lives. When we pretend otherwise, we risk making terrible, life-changing mistakes.

Armstrong's saga had a happy ending. Though she was upset by the experience and stopped blogging for several months afterwards, she ended up getting married and restarting her blog with a focus on her new family. Today she is a star in the burgeoning ranks of 'mommy bloggers' and her writing supports her house hold. Once a poster child for the wages of web indiscretion, she has become a virtuoso of managed self-revelation. What Armstrong has figured out is something we would all do well to remember: the web may allow us to say anything, but that doesn't mean we should.

31 Why does the writer describe a website about public check-ins in the first paragraph?

    A to reinforce the concerns already felt by some people

    B to remind readers to beware of false promises

    C to explain that such sites often have a hidden agenda

    D to show that the risks of internet use are sometimes overestimated

32 What is the writer's attitude to the online pioneers mentioned in the second paragraph?

    A He is concerned by the risks they took.

    B He appreciates their unprecedented achievements.

    C He admires their technical skills.

    D He is impressed by the extent of their cooperation.

33 What does the writer suggest about Justin Hall in the third paragraph?

    A He was unusually innovative in his approach.

    B His work was popular for the wrong reasons.

    C He inspired others writing in different fields of study.

    D His work displayed considerable literary skill.

34 What point is exemplified by the references to Hall's project in the fourth paragraph?

    A People usually dislike exhibitionists.

    B Someone's life can be a form of art.

    C Relationships are always a private matter.

    D Being too open may be counterproductive.

35 What does the account of Armstrong's later career suggest about blogging?

    A It is important to choose an appropriate audience.

    B It is possible to blog safely and successfully.

    C It is vital to consider the feelings of others.

    D It is best to avoid controversial subjects when blogging.

36 In this article, the writer's aim is to

    A illustrate a point.

    B defend a proposition.

    C describe developments.

    D compare arguments.

Part 6

You are going to read an article about a company which makes unusual bicycles. Seven paragraphs have been removed from the extract. Choose from the paragraphs **A–H** the one which fits each gap (**37–43**). There is one extra paragraph which you do not need to use. Mark your answers **on the separate answer sheet.**

Build it yourself at the UK's first bamboo bike workshop

A course at the Bamboo Bike Club, run by engineers James Marr and Ian McMillan,
buys you a computer-designed custom frame plus a fun weekend of bike-building

It's Saturday morning in Hackney Wick, east London, and apart from a mechanic deep in the bowels of a truck, the only sign of life among the small factories on a backstreet is a whine of machinery from an upper window – work has begun at Bamboo Bike Club, Britain's only bamboo bike-building course. I've gone along to watch the action.

37

There's a sense of energy and industry. And of fun. Woodwork class was never like this. Bamboo is one of the most interesting trends to emerge in bike construction. Names like Californian manufacturer Calfee Design or Yorkshire's Bamboo Bikes have revived a construction method pioneered as early as 1894. The problem for most cyclists is the price. A ready-made bamboo frame from these companies retails for $2,995, or £1,868.

38

Only after they had refined their research into a marketable product – James now tosses out phrases like 'close-noded thick-wall tubes' while talking about bamboo – did they realise they were on the wrong track. 'We realised we didn't want just to sell frames. We wanted to share the joy of making something; the craft of creating something unique and sustainable,' James explains.

39

The question for me, a king of the botch job – my terrible handiwork failures litter my house – was about quality. On day one, the boys explain how to select bamboo for strength and how to form strong joints before tubes are glued lightly in place in the workshop: first the front triangle composed of 40 mm diameter bamboo; then the thinner, more fiddly seat and the chain assembly. Alloy tubes are inserted for the handlebars, wheel forks and other parts which require the strength and precise engineering impossible in bamboo.

40

James and Ian buzz cheerfully between workbenches, supervising every cut, triple-checking every joint, and will take over if a task seems insurmountable. The self-build is half the attraction for most participants; it may be no coincidence that all those on this course were engineers. For the rest of us, Ian reassures that everyone messes up once or twice.

41

Sunday is a more relaxed day, mainly spent building the lugs. Or rather, wraps: hemp bindings wrapped around the joints and dropouts then glued with epoxy resin to form a strong bond that disperses loads evenly throughout the frame. With a final polymer coating for waterproofing, the bike is ready for wheels, brakes, gears, saddle and any other individual touches. And it is a bike built for the long haul, just as strong, the pair claim, as its metal equivalents.

42

Technical issues aside, how good does a bamboo bike look? Somewhat scruffy alongside professional frames, it turns out – the hemp weave can look a bit like parcel tape, for example. But there's no denying their individuality and that, say James and Ian, is the point.

43

They also cycle well. I take James's bike for a spin and the ride is light, stiff and smooth thanks to bamboo's ability to dampen vibration. Impressive, considering I target every pothole. 'Some people love the build, but for me these workshops come together when the bike is on the road,' James says. 'They're so light, so effortless to ride. So much fun to ride too – take a Harley-style retro bike, add 10 and you're still not close.' And the price? Less than £500.

A All this, together with the technical skill involved in using jigs, power tools and design blueprints, is a leap of faith for someone whose idea of DIY is flatpack furniture assembly. Accurate cutting for a clean joint can be tricky, for example.

B Personally though, I believe that any bicycle made from this kind of material should be a relaxed affair, something for cruising sedately around on rather than racing. I therefore plump for a frame that avoids the stiff angularity of my existing metal machine: a 'Classic English' giving a gentle, easy- going ride.

C Frames have been set up for the three custom bikes under construction. Bamboo has been selected from a stockpile. Now crossbars and seatposts are being cut according to the lengths specified on each design's blueprint.

D No problem – just get another piece and have another go. Such is the benefit of bamboo. Each length has been pre-checked for quality, so you get to indulge in frame aesthetics: plain bamboo, black or mottled.

E If Calfee and their like are safe, middle-of-the-road rock, then Bamboo Bike Club are the punks, the rebels; less up against the big names than creating bikes that embody the DIY spirit and that will engender more passion than the average factory-line model.

F It was this, plus the design challenge, that led James and Ian to spend years cooped up in a shed in Brecon, Wales. Their idea was to establish a boutique bamboo bike business with products within reach of the average cyclist.

G Ian has ridden his for over a year on a 16-mile commute, while James has failed to destroy one bike off-road over three months of testing. 'To be honest, our bikes are over-engineered – we use larger diameter tubes and over-thick bindings – but I prefer it like that,' James says.

H The outcome was something more community than company, and as such, the Bamboo Bike Club is still an occupation sandwiched between full-time jobs – James makes wind turbines and Ian is a civil engineer. But they seem to be on the right track, with monthly courses whose competitive price buys you a computer-designed custom bike frame plus a fun weekend of bike-building.

Part 7

You are going to read extracts from an introductory book about studying the law. For questions **44–53**, choose from the sections (**A–D**). The extracts may be chosen more than once. Mark your answers **on the separate answer sheet.**

In which extract are the following mentioned?

the relative frequency of certain types of legal cases	44
input by those who are not directly involved in a dispute	45
how common transactions assume certain guarantees	46
ascertaining the effectiveness of a legal system	47
determining the consequences of altering the legal system	48
the influence of popular depictions of the law	49
a reluctance to submit to formal legal processes	50
how a decentralised legal system depends on a feeling of reciprocity	51
the lack of drama in the way the law operates	52
the absence of a certain type of legal institution	53

Studying the law

A

Ordinary people regularly encounter law in a variety of circumstances. Freely-negotiated commercial contracts may bind them to act in particular ways. By becoming members of a sports club or a trade union they agree to comply with a set of rules. Sometimes these forms of law will use the courts to enforce their arrangements. In other cases privately-instituted adjudication bodies are established, a third party being appointed to decide whether an agreement or rule has been broken or not. These kinds of arrangements may seem very different from the normal idea of law, especially if law is thought of mainly in terms of the criminal law. However, it is possible to see law simply as a way of regulating our actions, of deciding what can be done and what cannot be done. Most laws are not about something spectacular but, rather, about the details of ordinary life. Every time a purchase is made, a contract is made. Both parties make promises about what they will do; one to hand over the goods, one to pay the price. In this and other ways, everybody is involved in law every day of their lives.

B

Legal rules can be divided up in many different ways. The rules show differences in purpose, in origin and form, in the consequences when they are breached, and in matters of procedure, remedies and enforcement. One of the most fundamental divisions in law is the division between criminal and civil law. Newcomers to the study of law tend to assume that criminal law occupies the bulk of a lawyer's caseload and of a law student's studies. This is an interesting by-product of the portrayal of the legal system by the media. Criminal law weighs very lightly in terms of volume when measured against non-criminal (that is, civil) law. There are more rules of civil law than there are of criminal law; more court cases involve breach of the civil law than that of the criminal law.

C

The term 'national law' is used to mean the internal legal rules of a particular country, in contrast to international law which deals with the external relationships of a state with other states. There is no world government or legislature issuing and enforcing laws to which all nations are subject. The international legal order has no single governing body and operates by agreement between states. This means that the creation, interpretation and enforcement of international law lie primarily in the hands of states themselves. Its scope and effectiveness depend on the sense of mutual benefit and obligation involved in adhering to the rules. Disputes about the scope and interpretation of international law are rarely resolved by the use of international courts or binding arbitration procedures of an international organisation. This is because submission to an international court or similar process is entirely voluntary and few states are likely to agree to this if there is a serious risk of losing their case or where important political or national interests are at stake.

D

One source of detailed information about the legal system is statistical analyses. Information about the number of cases handled by a court shows in specific terms what a court's workload is. Changes in these from year to year may indicate some effects of changes in the law and practice. Statistical tests can establish that there is a relationship, a correlation, between different things. For example, the length of a sentence for theft may correlate with the value of the items stolen or the experience of the judge who heard the case. This means that the sentence will be longer if, for example, more items are stolen or the judge is more experienced. A correlation can provide evidence for a theory. Such confirmation is important; without it we have little to establish the impact the law has, being forced to rely on individual instances of its application and having to assume that these have general truth. Empirical study of the operation of law may reveal areas of improvement. It can also confirm that, measured by particular standards, the courts are working well.

WRITING (1 hour 30 minutes)

Part 1

Read the two texts below.

Write an essay summarising and evaluating the key points from both texts. Use your own words throughout as far as possible, and include your own ideas in your answers.

Write your answer in **240–280** words.

1

Throwing things away

Every week many of us throw away a huge amount of stuff, ranging from packaging for food and plastic bottles to old newspapers and junk mail. Fortunately some, though not all, of this can be recycled successfully and both governments and private citizens seem to be doing their best to ensure that this happens nowadays. We should be careful not to congratulate ourselves too soon, however, because whether enough is being done is highly debatable. For example, the vast numbers of plastic bags used, many of which are not biodegradable, damage the environment, most notably the oceans, where they endanger marine life.

Communications technology

It seems that nowadays we keep electronic products such as mobile phones for only a short time, because we are bombarded with highly effective advertising that persuades us that we need to discard our present model in favour of the latest, improved device. Our willingness to discard such products may also be a consequence of the dizzying pace of technological change. We can hardly be expected to remain behind the times, and we naturally wish to keep up with the latest exciting features and developments in communications technology.

Write your **essay**.

Part 2

Write an answer to **one** of the questions **2–5** in this part. Write your answer in **280–320** words in an appropriate style.

---

2   A general interest magazine has recently published a feature entitled 'Taking risks makes life worth living'. The editor has asked readers to write in with their own experiences and views on the topic. You decide to write a letter briefly describing a risk you once took and its consequences. You should also discuss why some people are particularly attracted to taking risks and how this behaviour might be justified.

Write your **letter**.

3   Some bus services in your area are to be withdrawn, and the local council has asked people to submit reports for the council website on the impact this will have. You decide to submit a report on one bus service that is under consideration. Your report should briefly describe the route and explain its importance. You should also assess the role that a good transport system plays in either urban or rural areas.

Write your **report**.

4   A magazine is running a series of articles on people's experiences of being close to nature, for example, visits to beautiful lakes or mountains, or encounters with wildlife. You decide to write an article in which you briefly describe an experience you have had when you were close to nature, and explain what you learned from this. You should also evaluate the role that contact with nature plays in people's lives.

Write your **article**.

5   Write an answer to **one** of the following two questions based on **one** of the titles below. Write **5(a)** or **5(b)** at the beginning of your answer.

   (a)   Anne Tyler: *The Accidental Tourist*
        'Two of the most important influences in this book are a child we never meet – and a dog.' Write a review for your local college magazine of *The Accidental Tourist*. You should briefly explain this comment and analyse the roles of Ethan and Edward in the story as a whole.

        Write your **review**.

   (b)   Ann Patchett: *Bel Canto*
        An international literary magazine has asked readers to send in articles entitled 'Music is the food of love … ' with reference to the role of music in books they have read.

        You decide to write an article about *Bel Canto*, briefly describing Roxanne's role in the house and evaluating the connection between music and love in her relationships.

        Write your **article**.

LISTENING (40 minutes approximately)

Part 1

You will hear three different extracts.

For questions **1–6**, choose the answer (**A, B** or **C**) which fits best according to what you hear. There are two questions for each extract.

Extract One

You hear two colleagues discussing the work they are doing in a historic palace.

1 What is the man's role in the restoration work?

   A   managing the restoration being done
   B   researching how previous restoration was done
   C   assessing whether restoration needs to be done

2 How does the woman feel now about the purchase of an original dining table?

   A   impressed it was worth so much
   B   frustrated that it took so long to find it
   C   satisfied with the part she played

Extract Two

You hear part of an interview with a scientist who is talking about her research into primate communication.

3 The scientist compares the sounds primates make to human speech in order to illustrate

   A   the research methods scientists have used.
   B   a question scientists have been trying to solve.
   C   the huge variety in primate sounds.

4 The scientist thinks the reason that gelada monkeys are significant is because

   A   they use facial gestures in a similar way to humans.
   B   the types of sounds they make are similar to human speech.
   C   the rhythm of their vocalisation is similar to that of humans.

Extract Three

You hear a journalist talking about changes that have taken place over her professional lifetime.

5 What explanation does the journalist give for changes in the quality of news reports?

   A   the ease with which information can be manipulated
   B   the public demand for sensational images
   C   the value placed on real-time reporting

6 She refers to different ways of eating to suggest that readers of printed newspapers

   A   begin by selecting what interests them most.
   B   tackle content that is difficult.
   C   skim over the majority of topics.

Part 2

You will hear part of a lecture about an architect called Josh Keysall, who became famous for designing environmentally friendly houses known as Earthpods.

For questions **7–15**, complete the sentences with a word or short phrase.

Soon after graduating, Keysall thought up a successful way of providing

(7) .... in the construction of buildings.

In his first Earthpod, Keysall used **(8)** .... instead of bricks to make the walls.

The speaker says the Earthpods are passive solar buildings with walls which are like

(9) .... in the way they function.

Keysall uses the term **(10)** .... to describe the independence of his Earthpods from conventional energy sources.

An Earthpod originally used as a **(11)** .... in Switzerland was specially adapted for the climate.

In Belgium, safety regulations prevented Keysall from using

(12) .... to construct an Earthpod.

In the UK, an Earthpod project involved the protection of some

(13) .... living in the area.

Following complaints about defects such as **(14)** ...., Keysall lost his professional status.

A film called **(15)** .... has been made about Keysall's life, work and legal battles.

Part 3

You will hear part of an interview in which two academics, Julia Ford and Stuart Cameron, discuss human memory.

For questions **16–20**, choose the answer (**A**, **B**, **C** or **D**) which fits best according to what you hear.

16 Julia and Stuart both think that concerns about the reliability of shared memories are

    A over-emphasised in some studies.

    B reasonable in some situations.

    C underestimated by some psychologists.

    D unfounded in legal contexts.

17 What surprised Stuart about how older couples remembered information?

    A the marked difference in the success of their approach

    B the few signs of personal disagreement

    C the great variety in the memories recalled

    D the evidence of the use of similar processes.

18 Julia and Stuart agree that the least effective sharing of memories occurred when one person

    A ignored the knowledge of the other person.

    B tried to control the direction of the conversation.

    C knew a lot more about the topic than the other person.

    D contradicted information given by the other person.

19 Julia contrasts humans with animals in order to

    A illustrate human social independence.

    B suggest humans abuse their privileges.

    C emphasise the carelessness of some humans.

    D explain how humans are vulnerable.

20 When talking about the nature of change in human memory, Julia and Stuart reveal

    A their respect for art history.

    B their insistence on scientific evidence.

    C their interest in cultural explanations.

    D their differences regarding philosophical claims.

Part 4

You will hear five short extracts in which university students are talking about the profession they are training for.

TASK ONE

For questions **21–25**, choose from the list (**A–H**) how each speaker feels about their course.

TASK TWO

For questions **26–30**, choose from the list (**A–H**) what each speaker says about future prospects for those on the course.

While you listen, you must complete both tasks.

		TASK ONE		TASK TWO
A appreciative of its challenge			**A** Success is easier for those with good connections.	
B worried about falling behind with the practical aspects			**B** A good reputation can count for a lot.	
C surprised by its wider relevance	Speaker 1	21	**C** Related work may be difficult to find.	Speaker 1 □ 26
D frustrated at the lack of information	Speaker 2	22	**D** The job market is expected to grow in this area.	Speaker 2 □ 27
E pleased at having overcome a problem	Speaker 3	23	**E** A personal quality is needed that many lack.	Speaker 3 □ 28
F surprised at changes that have taken place	Speaker 4	24	**F** To get a well-paid position it is necessary to specialise.	Speaker 4 □ 29
G pleased with progress relative to others	Speaker 5	25	**G** Academic success is vital.	Speaker 5 □ 30
H concerned by the lack of support for others			**H** The first years of work are very stressful.	

SPEAKING (16 minutes)

There are two examiners. One (the interlocutor) conducts the test, providing you with the necessary materials and explaining what you have to do. The other examiner (the assessor) will be introduced to you, but then takes no further part in the interaction.

Part 1 (2 minutes)

The interlocutor first asks you and your partner a few questions which focus on information about yourselves.

Part 2 (4 minutes)

In this part of the test you and your partner are asked to talk together. The interlocutor places a set of pictures on the table in front of you. There may be only one picture in the set or as many as seven pictures. This stimulus provides the basis for a discussion. The interlocutor first asks an introductory question which focuses on two of the pictures (or in the case of a single picture, on aspects of the picture). After about a minute, the interlocutor gives you both a decision-making task based on the same set of pictures.

The pictures for Part 2 are on page C2 of the colour section.

Part 3 (10 minutes)

You are each given the opportunity to talk for two minutes, to comment after your partner has spoken and to take part in a more general discussion.

The interlocutor gives you a card with a question written on it and asks you to talk about it for two minutes. After you have spoken, the interlocutor asks you both another question related to the topic on the card, addressing your partner first. This procedure is repeated, so that your partner receives a card and speaks for two minutes and a follow-up question is asked.

Finally, the interlocutor asks some further questions, which lead to a discussion on a general theme related to the subjects already covered in Part 3.

The cards for Part 3 are on pages C6–C7 of the colour section.

Test 2

READING AND USE OF ENGLISH (1 hour 30 minutes)

Part 1

For questions **1–8**, read the text below and decide which answer (**A, B, C** or **D**) best fits each gap.

Mark your answers **on the separate answer sheet**.

There is an example at the beginning (**0**).

Example:

0   **A**   distinguish   **B**   sense   **C**   feel   **D**   identify

0	A	B	C	D
	▭	▬	▭	▭

The way we see the things around us

'Pastry,' once wrote a cookery expert, 'like horses and children, seems to **(0)** .... if you are afraid of it and plays up **(1)** ....' Had she been writing today, she might well have mentioned that computers are just the same. Like small children, they do not **(2)** .... well to force, and just as one way of **(3)** .... with a fractious child is to send it to its room to **(4)** .... off, so quite often, if the machine is giving trouble, the first thing to try is simply switching it off and doing something else; quite why the machine works **(5)** .... when you boot it up again I have no idea.

(6) .... human emotions and feelings to inanimate objects is, of course, extremely unscientific; it's only those who don't understand machines who believe that they behave like people. But I would **(7)** .... that, although treating machines like people may be misguided, it is **(8)** ...., in general, to treating people like machines.

28

1 **A** correspondingly   **B** similarly   **C** accordingly   **D** appropriately

2 **A** respond   **B** reply   **C** adapt   **D** answer

3 **A** reacting   **B** dealing   **C** handling   **D** bargaining

4 **A** ease   **B** calm   **C** quieten   **D** cool

5 **A** perfectly   **B** completely   **C** reasonably   **D** competently

6 **A** Associating   **B** Attributing   **C** Accrediting   **D** Admitting

7 **A** support   **B** decide   **C** confirm   **D** maintain

8 **A** desirable   **B** preferable   **C** advisable   **D** suitable

Part 2

For questions **9–16**, read the text below and think of the word which best fits each space. Use only **one** word in each space. There is an example at the beginning (**0**). Write your answers **IN CAPITAL LETTERS on the separate answer sheet.**

Example: | **0** | A | W | A | Y | | | | | | | | | | | | | | | |

Driverless cars

Driverless cars would of course, do **(0)** ……… with the stress of driving, allowing their occupants to read, browse the internet or take a nap, and they would also eliminate accidents caused by human error.

The benefits would go **(9)** ……… comfort and safety, however, since they would also revolutionise transport and urban planning. Traffic lights and road signs would no **(10)** ……… be needed. Different autonomous vehicles on the road would be able to coordinate their movements, and travel **(11)** ……… close formation, so that traffic would be kept flowing without interruption, **(12)** ……… journeys quicker and road use more efficient. On the one hand, this might mean that cities got bigger, as a **(13)** ……… of commuting times being reduced; on the **(14)** ………, they could become denser, with houses in the space previously dedicated to roads.

It may all sound **(15)** ……… science fiction, but much of the technology needed to turn ordinary vehicles into self-driving ones already exists. Almost **(16)** ……… car makers are developing systems which will in effect turn cars into autonomous robots.

Part 3

For questions **17–24**, read the text below. Use the word given in capitals at the end of some of the lines to form a word that fits in the space in the same line. There is an example at the beginning (**0**). Write your answers **IN CAPITAL LETTERS on the separate answer sheet**.

Example: | 0 | M | I | C | R | O | S | C | O | P | I | C | | | | | | |

Exploring the oceans

A million new species of **(0)** .... sea life have recently been observed for **SCOPE**

the first time, promising **(17)** .... about the marine ecosystem that could **REVEAL**

(18) .... our understanding of the impact of climate change on the oceans. **REVOLVE**

Each new life form was observed in the **(19)** .... of the Pacific and Atlantic **DEEP**

oceans by the research vessel, the *Tara*, which was a **(20)** .... small ship to be **COMPARE**

undertaking a mission on this scale.

The expedition's **(21)** .... show for the first time the quite remarkable diversity **FIND**

of tiny plankton that are a vital food source for fish and whales. In total, 1.5 million

species of microorganisms were recorded – **(22)** .... more than previously **SIGNIFY**

thought – and some of these were extraordinarily beautiful.

Worryingly, the scientists report that the oceans are becoming more acidic, and

this will continue if **(23)** .... of carbon dioxide increase, or even if they remain **EMIT**

at current levels. Since these organisms are sensitive to acid, they could become

(24) .... species in the future. **DANGER**

Part 4

For questions **25–30**, complete the second sentence so that it has a similar meaning to the first sentence, using the word given. **Do not change the word given**. You must use between **three** and **eight** words, including the word given. Here is an example (**0**).

Example:

0 Do you mind if I watch you while you paint?

objection

Do you .... you while you paint?

0	*have any objection to my watching*

Write **only** the missing words **on the separate answer sheet**.

---

25 Sam moved house only because he disliked commuting.

dislike

But for his .... moved house.

26 Katy didn't seem nervous, even though she was making her speech without notes.

sign

Katy ...., even though she was making her speech without notes.

27 The manager said he was extremely confident that his team could cope with the challenges ahead.

every

The manager said he .... to cope with the challenges ahead.

28 More and more tourists are visiting the ancient towns in the mountains.

growth

There .... tourists visiting the ancient towns in the mountains.

29 I don't think Harriet has any idea how difficult it is to use this apparatus.

involved

I don't think Harriet has any idea .... this apparatus.

30 Because the room is not available today, they have rearranged the meeting for next week.

put

Because the room is not available today, the meeting .... next week.

Part 5

You are going to read an article about the advantages and disadvantages of pessimistic and optimistic attitudes. For questions **31–36**, choose the answer (**A**, **B**, **C** or **D**) which you think fits best according to the text. Mark your answers **on the separate answer sheet.**

Are you an Optimist or a Pessimist?

*Whichever you are, a new book reveals that you can learn
a lot from attempting the opposite attitude.*

As a nation, the British are not a very optimistic bunch. When we were first granted the honour of hosting the 2012 Olympic Games, according to an opinion poll at the time, 55 per cent of us were more concerned about the likely impact on the transport network while the Games were on than with celebrating the arrival of the greatest show on Earth. But alongside this type of staunch pessimism resides an unsettling feeling that we should be more positive. We are always trying to dislodge each other's pessimism. Test it for yourself: sit gloomily in a public place and see how long it takes before a smiling passer-by says, 'Cheer up, it might never happen!' or offers one of those trite aphorisms about 'looking on the bright side' or 'clouds having silver linings'.

The self-help industry rakes in billions through peddling hope and positive thinking. But can a positive outlook really improve our lives? How can optimism make people more trustworthy, or sports events more successful? It can't, says Professor Elaine Fox, a neuroscientist who recently published a book called *Rainy Brain, Sunny Brain* about our ambivalent feelings of optimism and pessimism. Our negativity is the response of a rational mind and positivity is a delusion, she says, and for most of us they both act to balance us out. 'Positivity is a delusion. But it is a useful delusion. If we didn't have some sort of optimism we wouldn't ever get out of bed in the morning. But pessimism has its place,' she says.

So, when we think positively, are we just tricking ourselves that things will get better? It's a little more complicated than that, says Professor Fox. 'Where self-help books say "just think happy thoughts" it doesn't work.' But some degree of optimism can work to our advantage, because if we feel more positive, we will take more positive actions. 'Optimism gives you a sense of control,' she explains. So, to return to the example of the Olympics, if we had just repeated the mantra, 'the Olympics will be amazing, the Olympics will be amazing' it wouldn't have made it happen. In the event we actually did respond positively to them, but by taking the kind of actions – buying tickets to events, or getting involved as volunteers – that meant we ended up loving the whole experience.

More dramatically, positive thoughts can have concrete health benefits and can help us through certain situations, Professor Fox explains. In experiments on pain in which students are asked to keep their hands in a bucket of ice water for as long as they can stand it, students who believe they have been given a painkiller, but have in actual fact just been given a sugar pill, will keep their hand in longer than those who aren't given anything. Scans of their brains show they actually produce a surge of dopamine, a so-called 'happy' chemical, which combats the pain.

'Thomas Edison, the famous American inventor, said, "If I find 10,000 ways something won't work, I haven't failed. I am not discouraged, because every wrong attempt discarded is another step forward." In general, optimists will try harder and spend longer on something than pessimists,' says Professor Fox. 'They also believe they have some control over their life, and that's why they tend to be more successful.'

But don't shrug off your grumpy cynicism just yet. Professor Fox says a healthy dose of negativity can help us out, too. 'The amygdala – the fear system in our brain that helps us detect threat and danger – is really at the root of pessimism. Pessimism helps us suss out danger in our lives.' And although most of us are unlikely to need this reaction the same way our caveman ancestors did – for fight-or-flight reactions – fear is still a useful trait. 'A pessimistic outlook would work if you were setting up your own business,' says Professor Fox, 'to identify risk and avoid it.' So, there is a place for pessimism. 'They say the aeroplane was invented by an optimist and the parachute was invented by a pessimist. That's the reason I called the book *Rainy Brain, Sunny Brain*, because we need both.' Anticipate sunshine, but carry an umbrella and you should get along just fine.

31 The writer says that British attitudes to the 2012 Olympic Games

    A illustrated an underlying mindset.

    B contradicted stereotypes of national character.

    C reflected a shift in public opinion.

    D indicated the dangers of ambivalence.

32 In the second paragraph, we learn that Professor Fox believes being optimistic

    A is more desirable than being pessimistic.

    B is a necessary counter to our negativity.

    C is likely to lead to unrealistic expectations.

    D is as natural a quality as pessimism.

33 What does Professor Fox suggest about positive thinking in the third paragraph?

    A It is difficult to find any sensible advice about it.

    B It is ineffective unless carefully planned.

    C It is desirable as it will lead to material benefits.

    D It is likely to be the basis for practical achievement.

34 What is the writer illustrating by using the phrase 'the Olympics will be amazing'?

    A the futility of merely thinking positively

    B the way that positive thoughts can motivate people

    C the importance of overcoming negative thinking

    D the fact that people can be trained to think in certain ways

35 What point is exemplified by the reference to Thomas Edison?

    A In order to be successful, we have to experience failure.

    B Optimists gain success through persistence.

    C Successful people are often unwilling to work for others.

    D Success comes more easily to optimists than pessimists.

36 In the final paragraph, it is said that the invention of the parachute

    A was a necessary consequence of the invention of the aeroplane.

    B proved that humans always tend to fear the worst.

    C was comparable to someone starting a company.

    D demonstrated a readiness to confront the idea of risk.

Part 6

You are going to read an article about a tourist destination in Australia. Seven paragraphs have been removed from the extract. Choose from the paragraphs **A–H** the one which fits each gap (**37–43**). There is one extra paragraph which you do not need to use. Mark your answers **on the separate answer sheet.**

Visiting Uluru

One day in 1874, an explorer, Ernest Giles, struggled up a small hill and was confronted with a sight such as he could never have dreamed of finding. Before him, impossibly imposing, stood the most singular monolith on earth, the great red rock now known as Uluru. Hastening to report the find, he was informed that a man named William Gosse had chanced upon it a few days ahead of him and had already named it Ayers Rock after the South Australia governor.

37

So you are aware, as you drive to the park entrance, that you have driven 1,300 miles to look at something you have seen portrayed a thousand times already. In consequence, your mood as you approach this famous monolith is restrained, unexpectant – pessimistic even. And then you see it, and you are instantly transfixed. There, in the middle of a memorable and imposing emptiness, stands an eminence of exceptional nobility and grandeur, 1,150 feet high, a mile and a half long, five and a half miles around.

38

It's not that Uluru is bigger than you had supposed or more perfectly formed or in any way different from the impression you had created in your mind, but the very opposite. It is exactly what you expected it to be. You *know* this rock. You know it in a way that has nothing to do with calendars and the covers of souvenir books.

39

It is a motion much too faint to be understood or interpreted, but somehow you sense that this large, brooding, hypnotic presence has an importance to you at the species level – perhaps even at a sort of tadpole level – and that in some way your visit here is more than happenstance.

40

I'm suggesting nothing here, but I will say that if you were an intergalactic traveller who had broken down

in our solar system, the obvious directions to rescuers would be: 'Go to the third planet and fly around till you see the big red rock. You can't miss it.' If ever on earth they dig up a 150,000-year-old rocket ship from the Galaxy Zog, this is where it will be. I'm not saying I expect it to happen; not saying that at all. I'm just observing that if I were looking for an ancient starship, this is where I would start digging.

41

You realize that you could spend quite a lot of time – possibly a worryingly large amount of time; possibly a sell-your-house-and-move-here-to-live-in-a-tent amount of time – just looking at the rock, gazing at it from many angles, never tiring of it. You can see yourself hanging out with much younger visitors and telling them: 'And the amazing thing is that every day it's different, you know what I'm saying? It's never the same rock twice. That's right, my friend – you put your finger on it there. It's awesome. It's an awesome thing.'

42

Instead, we stopped at the visitors' centre for a cup of coffee and to look at the displays, which were all to do with interpretations of the Dreamtime – the Aborigines' traditional conception of how the earth was formed and operates. There was nothing instructive in a historical or geological sense, which was disappointing because I was curious to know what Uluru is doing there. How do you get the biggest rock in existence onto the middle of an empty plain?

43

Afterwards we had one last drive around the rock before heading back to the lonely highway. We had been at the site for barely two hours, obviously not nearly enough time, but I realized as I turned around in my seat to watch it shrinking into the background behind us that there never could be enough, and I felt moderately comforted by that thought.

A It is less red than photographs have led you to expect but in every other way more arresting than you could ever have supposed. I have discussed this since with many other people, nearly all of whom agreed that they approached Uluru with a kind of fatigue, and were left amazed in a way they could not adequately explain.

B By the time you finally get there you are already a little sick of it. You can't go a day in Australia without seeing it four or five or six times – on postcards, on travel posters, on the cover of picture books – and as you get nearer, the frequency of exposure increases.

C Climbing up takes several hours and much exertion. Even when it's not too hot, lots of people get in trouble. Just the day before a Canadian had had to be rescued off a ledge from which he could not get either up or down. Fortunately, they close it to climbers when the weather is really warm, as it was this day.

D It is grounded in something much more elemental. In some odd way that you don't understand and can't begin to articulate you feel an acquaintance with it – a familiarity on an unfamiliar level. Somewhere in the deep sediment of your being some long-dormant fragment of memory has twitched or stirred.

E In fact, it is almost 300 miles across a largely featureless tract. Uluru's glory is that it stands alone in a boundless emptiness, but it does mean that you have to really want to see it; it's not something you're going to pass on the way to the beach.

F It turns out that Uluru is what is known as a bornhardt: a hunk of weather-resistant rock left standing when all else around it has worn away; but nowhere else on earth has one hunk of rock been left in such dramatic and solitary splendour or assumed such a pleasing smooth symmetry.

G I'm not saying that any of this is so. I'm just saying that this is how you feel. The other thought that strikes you – that struck me anyway – is that Uluru is not merely a splendid and mighty monolith, but also an extremely distinctive one.

H Quite apart from that initial shock of indefinable recognition, there is also the fact that Uluru is totally arresting. You cannot and don't want to stop looking at it. As you draw closer, it becomes even more interesting. It is less regular than you had imagined. There are more curves and more irregularities than are evident from even a couple of hundred yards away.

Part 7

You are going to read an article about the present-day importance of the moon landings. For questions **44–53**, choose from the sections (**A–E**). The sections may be chosen more than once. Mark your answers **on the separate answer sheet.**

In which section are the following mentioned?

a tribute to the ambitions of the space programme	**44**
the accelerated development of technology	**45**
a lack of encouragement to continue with a project	**46**
various factors which made a task particularly challenging	**47**
an individual example of the inspiring effects of Apollo	**48**
an event marking the end of an era	**49**
a spirited response to a seemingly impossible provocation	**50**
the effects of the space programme on attitudes to sharing information	**51**
a radical alteration of existing technology	**52**
an influential combination of factors affecting the space programme	**53**

Living in the Moon's Shadow

More than forty years on, why the moon landings are still having an impact today

A

On December 19, 1972, a sonic boom above the South Pacific signaled the completion of the Apollo program, as a tiny space capsule burst back through the blue sky. On board were the last three astronauts to visit the moon. The space race has changed the course of human history far more profoundly than anyone could have predicted in 1961, when a new president challenged America to land a man on the moon and return him safely to the Earth. No one present knew how to make it happen. But that wasn't going to stop them rising to President Kennedy's dare.

B

As progress in human space flight sped up through the 1960s, Ph.D. intake at American universities, particularly in the field of physics, increased almost threefold. Apollo was making America cleverer. Within weeks of Kennedy's speech, the Massachusetts Institute of Technology (MIT) was asked to work out the small matter of helping astronauts make a soft landing on a moving target hurtling through space 250,000 miles from Earth. To assist them in this, a small, lightweight computer was proposed by MIT. In the early '60s, computers often took up entire rooms. To miniaturize one enough to pack it into a modestly-sized craft they'd need new technology, so they turned to a brand new arrival on the technology scene: the integrated circuit.

C

Only a few companies were experimenting with these new micro-electronic components at the time; keen to help them perfect the performance of these novel miniature circuits, NASA ordered one million of them. The agency really only needed a few hundred, but, aware that they would be betting the lives of their astronauts on them, they were keen to make sure the manufacturers could make them as reliable as possible. Such a financial kickstart to a fledgling industry, coupled with another gift of Apollo — inspiration — would prove to be powerful drivers for technological change in the decades that followed. Those graduating across the world in the '70s and '80s had watched Apollo's engineers dream the impossible and then build it. As an act of human ingenuity, Apollo made them giddy, intoxicated on admiration and inspiration. As William Bainbridge put it in his book 'The Spaceflight Revolution', Apollo was 'a grand attempt to reach beyond the world of mundane life and transcend the ordinary limits of human existence through accomplishment of the miraculous – a story of engineers who tried to reach the heavens.'

D

Many of the people who have built the new tools of the Internet and the technological infrastructure that underpins it cite Apollo as their motivator. Professor Sir Martin Sweeting founded the world-renowned small satellite company SSTL, which revolutionized the industry. 'Apollo started me on this whole pathway of getting involved in space,' says Sweeting. 'The idea of being able to participate in something as exciting as a lunar landing, it stimulated an ambition, the dream of building my own satellite with my friends.' The idea of a small private enterprise launching a satellite was considered pretty crazy at the time, he points out. 'After building the first one, I had a lot of advice to go out and get a proper job. I'm sure that without Apollo I would have followed a more conventional career.'

E

Former NASA flight director Glynn Lunney witnessed the trickle-down straight from Apollo to the rest of us. 'We were asking people to do things 10 or 20 years ahead of when they would otherwise have done them. And they knew it. They stepped up to it and succeeded. Today's cell phones, wireless equipment, tablet computers and so on are a result of the fact that the country did this high-tech thing and made this large portfolio of technologies available.' Today's population, over half of whom weren't born when those last astronauts returned from the moon, use these inventions to communicate with each other freely and without a thought for geographical and cultural differences. The gifts of Apollo continue to ripple down the decades, and still have the power to unite and inspire us.

WRITING (1 hour 30 minutes)

Part 1

Read the two texts below.

Write an essay summarising and evaluating the key points from both texts. Use your own words throughout as far as possible, and include your own ideas in your answers.

Write your answer in **240–280** words.

1

Being at home

For some people, it is only at home that they can truly relax. It is the place they go to to recover from both the excitements and the stress of their everyday life: the noisy hubbub of the city, the pressures of study and work, and the busy commute through rush-hour traffic. They appreciate the opportunity to reflect on all that has happened that day. They can contemplate the day's significant events either in the peace and quiet of their own room or through participating in a discussion over a meal.

Home and away

For many of us, life at home can be rather restrictive, or simply dull, so we escape to public places where we can socialise and be ourselves, such as cafés and coffee bars. Yet home is still a place where people can express their personalities. The choice of furniture, the colour scheme, and the paintings or posters displayed on the walls, will all say a great deal about the person who lives there. Visiting a friend's home for the first time may well reveal aspects of their personality which were previously unknown to us.

Write your **essay**.

Part 2

Write an answer to **one** of the questions **2–5** in this part. Write your answer in **280–320** words in an appropriate style.

---

2   You have recently worked as a volunteer, coaching teenagers at a sports camp designed to encourage young people to take up new sports. The organisers have asked you to write a report for the website. You should briefly describe your responsibilities as a coach for two different sports. You should also evaluate how valuable the sports camp was for the teenagers overall and recommend how it could be improved in future.

Write your **report**.

3   You have recently read some letters in a magazine discussing the question 'What are good manners?'. The magazine has invited readers to join the debate. You decide to write a letter in which you briefly describe one or two examples of what you consider to be good manners, explaining why behaving politely in those particular situations is necessary. You should also evaluate just how important good manners are nowadays.

Write your **letter**.

4   A film magazine has invited readers to submit reviews of films which are set in the future, but deal with themes relevant to today's world, such as our relationship with technology or environmental problems. You decide to submit a review briefly describing such a film and explaining why its themes are relevant today. You should also consider how important it is for films set in the future to say something about contemporary society.

Write your **review**.

5   Write an answer to **one** of the following two questions based on **one** of the titles below. Write **5(a)** or **5(b)** at the beginning of your answer.

(a)   Tracy Chevalier: *Girl with a Pearl Earring*
   'The earring would complete the painting. It would also put me on the street.'
   Your class tutor has asked you to write an essay assessing the significance of the pearl earrings in Griet's story, and explaining the way in which the earrings contribute to her losing her position in the Vermeer household.

   Write your **essay**.

(b)   Tobias Hill: *The Cryptographer*
   An English language magazine is running a series of articles dealing with the theme of money, and has asked its readers to send in articles for the series. You decide to write an article considering the importance of money in the relationship between John Law and Anna Moore in *The Cryptographer*. You should also explain why you think an article about this novel would be worth including in the series.

   Write your **article**.

LISTENING (40 minutes approximately)

Part 1

You will hear three different extracts. For questions **1–6**, choose the answer (**A**, **B** or **C**) which fits best according to what you hear.

There are two questions for each extract.

Extract One

You hear a well-known scientist giving a talk to a group of science graduates at their graduation ceremony.

1 Why does he mention the field of climate science?

   A   to emphasise the importance of examining data carefully
   B   to warn about the dangers of ignoring the evidence
   C   to suggest that some subjects are more controversial than others

2 What is the aim of his talk?

   A   to point out the value of sharing scientific knowledge
   B   to highlight what is most relevant in scientific study
   C   to criticise the way much scientific data is reported

Extract Two

You hear part of an interview with a psychologist on the subject of memory.

3 What is the psychologist's attitude to people who cannot forget?

   A   He criticises their limitations.
   B   He understands their uncertainty.
   C   He envies their ability.

4 The psychologist contrasts human memory and computer memory in order to

   A   demonstrate the versatility of human memory.
   B   emphasise the capacity of computer memory.
   C   question the provisional nature of perception.

Extract Three

You hear two media studies lecturers comparing electronic readers and printed materials.

5 Which aspect of printed books do they agree about?

    A   their practical inconvenience
    B   their physical appeal
    C   their environmental cost

6 What is the man doing when he refers to newspapers?

    A   deliberating on their future
    B   defending their role
    C   predicting their disappearance

Part 2

You will hear a student called Tom giving a presentation about non-native species of animals in Australia, and the problems they cause.

For questions **7–15**, complete the sentences with a word or short phrase.

Rabbits introduced from Europe are widespread in Australia except in regions where

(7) .... is present.

According to Tom, rabbits' feeding habits mean that foods such as

(8) .... are unavailable for native Australian birds.

An introduced species known as the cane toad can kill (9) ....

as well as smaller creatures with its poison.

Camels were introduced to Australia to carry supplies to (10) ....

in remote desert areas.

Australian camels particularly enjoy eating the (11) ....

of the apricot tree.

When water is scarce, camels may destroy village (12) ....

in poor communities.

It is too expensive to use (13) .... as a widespread means of
controlling invasive species.

Successful control measures have been implemented on one

(14) .... but other places are more difficult.

In Australia, (15) .... is in place to prevent the

problem from getting worse.

Part 3

You will hear part of an interview with two British architects, Malcolm Fletcher and Alison Brooks, about the design of new low-cost housing.

For questions **16–20**, choose the answer (**A, B, C** or **D**) which fits best according to what you hear.

16 What view is expressed about the government's plans to build houses on greenfield sites?

    A   Opposition groups are unlikely to have any real influence.

    B   It may be possible to create space by demolishing some existing buildings.

    C   There is a more important priority than preserving the countryside.

    D   New developments should show continuity with what has gone before.

17 What does Malcolm regard as special about the Newhall housing development in Essex?

    A   the involvement of local people in the planning process

    B   the unusual attitude of the original landowners

    C   the good relationship between the builders and the architect

    D   the freedom given to the designers

18 The aspect of Margaret Gibbs's houses which both Alison and Malcolm appreciate is

    A   their visual appeal.

    B   their generous dimensions.

    C   their structural strength.

    D   their internal layout.

19 When designing the space around the Essex houses, Margaret Gibbs

    A   attempted to integrate homes with recreational areas.

    B   conceded to the general demand for a garden.

    C   allowed a bigger external area than usual.

    D   aimed to safeguard the inhabitants' privacy.

20 What do Malcolm and Alison agree about the aesthetic qualities of buildings?

    A   Architectural form may sometimes take precedence over function.

    B   Beauty is an intrinsic aspect of good architecture.

    C   There is little consensus concerning what constitutes good style.

    D   Popular notions of good taste inevitably change over time.

Part 4

You will hear five short extracts in which people talk about academic conferences they have attended.

TASK ONE

For questions **21–25**, choose from the list (**A–H**) the reason each speaker gives for wanting to attend an academic conference.

TASK TWO

For questions **26–30**, choose from the list (**A–H**) how each speaker felt about the first presenter.

While you listen, you must complete both tasks.

A to learn about new trends	A disappointed by his lack of substance
B to listen to a celebrated speaker	B impressed by his claims
C to gain inspiration	C sceptical about his research results
D to re-connect with old friends	D amused by his anecdotes
E to discuss shared problems	E embarrassed by his hesitations
F to present a paper	F bored by his repetitions
G to enjoy a perk	G concerned by his inaccuracy
H to meet publishers	H annoyed by his original ideas

Speaker 1	21		Speaker 1	26
Speaker 2	22		Speaker 2	27
Speaker 3	23		Speaker 3	28
Speaker 4	24		Speaker 4	29
Speaker 5	25		Speaker 5	30

SPEAKING (16 minutes)

There are two examiners. One (the interlocutor) conducts the test, providing you with the necessary materials and explaining what you have to do. The other examiner (the assessor) will be introduced to you, but then takes no further part in the interaction.

Part 1 (2 minutes)

The interlocutor first asks you and your partner a few questions which focus on information about yourselves.

Part 2 (4 minutes)

In this part of the test you and your partner are asked to talk together. The interlocutor places a set of pictures on the table in front of you. There may be only one picture in the set or as many as seven pictures. This stimulus provides the basis for a discussion. The interlocutor first asks an introductory question which focuses on two of the pictures (or in the case of a single picture, on aspects of the picture). After about a minute, the interlocutor gives you both a decision-making task based on the same set of pictures.

The pictures for Part 2 are on page C3 of the colour section.

Part 3 (10 minutes)

You are each given the opportunity to talk for two minutes, to comment after your partner has spoken and to take part in a more general discussion.

The interlocutor gives you a card with a question written on it and asks you to talk about it for two minutes. After you have spoken, the interlocutor asks you both another question related to the topic on the card, addressing your partner first. This procedure is repeated, so that your partner receives a card and speaks for two minutes and a follow-up question is asked.

Finally, the interlocutor asks some further questions, which lead to a discussion on a general theme related to the subjects already covered in Part 3.

The cards for Part 3 are on pages C6–C7 of the colour section.

Test 3

READING AND USE OF ENGLISH (1 hour 30 minutes)

Part 1

For questions **1–8**, read the text below and decide which answer (**A**, **B**, **C** or **D**) best fits each gap.

Mark your answers **on the separate answer sheet**.

There is an example at the beginning (**0**).

0   **A** despatched   **B** launched   **C** commenced   **D** embarked

```
0 | A    B    C    D
  | ▭    ▬    ▭    ▭
```

A Cosmic Directory

Scientists at Puerto Rico University in Arecibo have recently **(0)** .... a cosmic directory that lists the planets and moons most likely to **(1)** .... alien life. They created the catalogue to make sense of the ever-increasing number of distant worlds that are visible with modern telescopes. They believe it will help astronomers, and others with an interest, to compare faraway worlds and keep **(2)** .... on the most habitable ones as researchers discover them.

The catalogue ranks the habitability of planets and moons according to three **(3)** ....: their surface temperature, their similarity to Earth and their capacity to **(4)** .... organisms that **(5)** .... at the bottom of the food chain. It suggests that among hundreds of candidates, only a few planets are **(6)** .... habitable, and gives high **(7)** .... for habitability to even fewer. The database also holds information on the **(8)** .... of the planets, their probable mass and the type and age of the stars they orbit.

1 **A** shield   **B** protect   **C** harbour   **D** safeguard

2 **A** eyes   **B** logs   **C** tabs   **D** check

3 **A** principles   **B** criteria   **C** concepts   **D** scales

4 **A** uphold   **B** maintain   **C** preserve   **D** sustain

5 **A** lurk   **B** loiter   **C** hide   **D** hover

6 **A** potentially   **B** plausibly   **C** predictably   **D** prospectively

7 **A** levels   **B** notes   **C** totals   **D** scores

8 **A** situation   **B** destination   **C** location   **D** orientation

Part 2

For questions **9–16**, read the text below and think of the word which best fits each space. Use only **one** word in each space. There is an example at the beginning (**0**). Write your answers **IN CAPITAL LETTERS on the separate answer sheet**

Example: | 0 | W | I | T | H | O | U | T | | | | | | | | | | |

Translation

In today's globalised world, the role the translator plays is, **(0)** .... a doubt, crucial. Each and **(9)** .... time translators set to work they have a heavy responsibility to communicate as accurately as possible. A poor translation might merely cause amusement, but at **(10)** ...., the consequences could sometimes be extremely serious.

There are a great many problems encountered in the translation process, some deriving **(11)** .... the grammatical differences between languages and others caused by idioms, not to mention highly specific cultural references that some argue, with good **(12)** .... perhaps, cannot be successfully translated.

It **(13)** .... without saying that translators should have a well-developed sensitivity to their mother tongue and the second language they work with. But whereas once they needed little **(14)** .... than exceptional linguistic skills, translators nowadays may require specialist knowledge of areas such as medicine, law or technology.

One factor they consider is how the translation sounds. Here, they may make **(15)** .... of strategies such as reading their translation aloud, thereby ensuring that words are not put in a sentence if, **(16)** .... individually accurate and appropriate, together they sound harsh or unpleasant.

Part 3

For questions **17–24**, read the text below. Use the word given in capitals at the end of some of the lines to form a word that fits in the space in the same line. There is an example at the beginning (**0**). Write your answers **IN CAPITAL LETTERS on the separate answer sheet**.

Example: | **0** | O | C | C | A | S | I | O | N | A | L | L | Y | | | | | | |

The need to read

All children **(0)** .... ask why we should bother reading. Now, 500 years after **OCCASION**

Gutenberg's printing press **(17)** .... reading, recent technological advances **DEMOCRACY**

mean psychologists may be able to find an answer. Using brain scans, they

have found we create mental simulations of situations **(18)** .... in a book and **COUNTER**

weave these together with real-life experiences to create a new way of thinking.

This is something many of us will understand **(19)** .... when we look back **INSTINCT**

and realise that an **(20)** .... book that we read in the past had an absolutely **STAND**

(21) .... effect on how we view the world. This transformation takes place **REVOLVE**

only when we lose ourselves **(22)** .... in a book. Studies have found this deep **CONDITION**

reading makes us more sympathetic, more alert to the **(23)** .... lives of others. **IN**

Here then is the irrefutable answer to our initial question, and it means that reading

must continue to be **(24)** .... in our culture. **BED**

Part 4

For questions **25–30**, complete the second sentence so that it has a similar meaning to the first sentence, using the word given. **Do not change the word given**. You must use between **three** and **eight** words, including the word given. Here is an example (**0**).

Example:

0 Do you mind if I watch you while you paint?

objection

Do you .... you while you paint?

0	*have any objection to my watching*

Write **only** the missing words **on the separate answer sheet**.

---

25 I don't think you'll find that many road atlases have such detailed maps.

few

I .... have such detailed maps.

26 The owner of the shop said that we didn't have to buy anything; we could just look round.

obligation

The owner of the shop said that we ....
a purchase; we could just look round.

27 Martin was too lazy to present any of his ideas at the meeting yesterday.

bothered

Martin .... forward any of his ideas at the meeting yesterday.

28 Once he'd handed in his entry, the only thing Tom could do was wait for the judge's decision.

nothing

Once he'd handed in his entry, there .... wait for the judge's decision.

29 Philip said that his friends were surprised when he suddenly decided to retire.

came

Philip said that his .... to his friends.

30 Susan doesn't intend to climb that mountain again.

has

Susan .... that mountain again.

Part 5

You are going to read an article about the 19th century French painter, Edouard Manet. For questions **31–36**, choose the answer (**A**, **B**, **C** or **D**) which you think fits best according to the text. Mark your answers **on the separate answer sheet**.

Manet: Portraying Life

A new exhibition of portraits by the great French painter, Manet

It is probably fair to say that Manet is not associated with the idea of penetrating portraiture. Although he used models as well as friends and insisted on painting only from prolonged, frequent sittings, it wasn't to dig deep into the psyche of his subjects, but to comment on their place through their appearance. All Manet's works were an assault. All, except for the flower paintings so derided by modern curators, were efforts to catch something of the contemporary world about him.

Very few of Manet's extensive output of portraits were commissioned. As the son of wealthy parents, he didn't need to earn his crust this way. Instead he painted his family, particularly his wife, the Dutch-born Suzanne Leenhoff, and her son, Léon, friends from among his wide circle of cultural contacts and professional models. What was it that he was seeking from these pictures? The simplest answer is 'realism', the observation of what was new and contemporary, which his mentor, the poet and critic Charles Baudelaire, proclaimed as the true test of modern art. Realism meant not just painting accurately from life, but stripping art of all the connotations of moral lesson and monumentality found in traditional art. Its heroes would become the man about town, the observer, the dandy.

But realism in portraiture for Manet was never merely a matter of recording the face and figure with verisimilitude. 'I cannot do anything without the model,' declared Manet. 'I do not know how to invent … . If I amount to anything today, I put it down to precise interpretation and faithful analysis.' But it was the 'interpretation' and 'analysis' that made him so different. With men it was to convey what they meant for the world about them. His portrait of Zacharie Astruc, the writer and critic who had done much to support him in his early years, is divided into two parts. On the right, Astruc sits somewhat pompously, his hand thrust into his jacket, while to the left is seen his wife in the kitchen, along with the symbols of the domestic life which underpins him. The portrait of Emile Zola, another great supporter, arranges the novelist with the attributes of his art criticism, an open book on Spanish art in his hand and a Japanese print above his desk.

With women it is quite different. Manet was clearly entranced by them, soaking up their vivacity, admiring their poise and revelling in a pretty face. It doesn't appear to have been predatory. Indeed the most touching pictures in the exhibition remain those of his wife, whom he painted more often and for longer than any other sitter; she is depicted at the piano, stroking the cat, resting in the conservatory. The plump and humorous face is always done with fondness, the background painted with quick, fleeting brushstrokes that envelop the sitter in the flowers around her or the dress she is wearing.

For Manet, dress was an assertion of modernity, a way of depicting the modern bourgeois woman who was emerging from the constraints of an aristocratic past. But, going round these galleries, it is difficult not to believe that he thought women the better, or at least the more life-enhancing, of the species. It is noticeable that in almost all the portraits of couples or couples with children – in the rather touching portrait of *The Monet Family in Their Garden at Argenteuil* and *In the Garden* of 1870 – it is the women who take the foremost role. It's more than their attractions and the dress; it's that Manet looks on them as the future more than the men in the background.

In Manet's portraiture, the parts don't add up to a whole. His efforts to start each picture anew don't make for an easy synthesis and, as such, gallery curators struggle to categorise them. A gathering of these varied and sometimes uneven works can't express all of the man. For that you really do need his bigger set pieces. This exhibition is not a gathering of masterpieces. Nor is it a comprehensive showing of his portraiture, given the paucity of the borrowings from France. But what you have is the outpouring of one of the towering geniuses of art who stood each time before his canvas with a subject, thought and thought about what he wanted to say and then worked to express it. Forget the whole, just look at the individual works and feel the mind behind them.

31 How does the writer say Manet's portraiture differed from that found in traditional art?

    A It was less commercial in style.

    B It demonstrated superior technical ability.

    C It was non-judgemental in approach.

    D It showed the influence of a literary movement.

32 According to the writer, Manet believed he was successful because he

    A had worked with the right people.

    B tried to convey his ideas accurately.

    C could see his subjects as they saw themselves.

    D was capable of highly life-like portraits.

33 References to the portraits of Astruc and Zola suggest Manet's

    A disdain for self-important men.

    B belief in the importance of context.

    C idea that nobody is beyond criticism.

    D view that all men are basically the same.

34 What do Manet's paintings of his wife show the viewer?

    A the way he felt about women in general

    B the important role his wife played in furthering his career

    C the variety of locations in which he enjoyed painting

    D the ability he had to capture the appearance of a sitter

35 Why does the writer think that Manet's portraits are problematic for gallery curators?

    A There is no common element running through them.

    B They are not sufficiently consistent in style.

    C They do not represent the true man behind them.

    D There are no truly outstanding pieces among them.

36 What does the writer conclude about the exhibition?

    A It tells us more about Manet than is obvious at first sight.

    B It gives an insight into the total commitment of a great painter.

    C It provides some serious challenges for the viewer.

    D It proves that art cannot be appreciated without understanding the artist.

Part 6

You are going to read an extract from a book about a trip to the country of Malawi. Seven paragraphs have been removed from the extract. Choose from the paragraphs **A–H** the one which fits each gap (**37–43**). There is one extra paragraph which you do not need to use. Mark your answers **on the separate answer sheet.**

Lake Malawi's lost resort

Novelist **Marina Lewycka** *reveals how getting lost in the African bush led her to find paradise by Lake Malawi*

It's easy to get off the beaten track in Malawi. In fact it can be difficult to stay on it, as we found three years ago when we were driving up the lake road from Salima towards Nkhata Bay for a week's holiday, in my daughter's old low-slung Nissan Bluebird, her boyfriend at the wheel.

| 37 | |

It became obvious that we weren't going to get to Nkhata Bay, and we'd have to stop somewhere overnight. We drove to a couple of upmarket lodges, but they were closed, or full, or just didn't like the look of us. We were directed to other, more remote places, which either didn't exist, or were also full; we were beginning to get worried.

| 38 | |

After a kilometre or so, it divided into a number of less distinct ones. They were definitely not beaten – they were hardly more than faint trails. There was no light ahead – in fact, there was no light anywhere, apart from the stars, which hung so close and bright you almost felt you could reach up and pick them out of the sky like low-hanging fruit.

| 39 | |

Beyond the narrow beam of our headlights, it was pitch black. All around us were prickly bushes, their vague menacing shapes blocking out the lie of the land. Swarms of mosquitoes smelled our fear, and swooped.

| 40 | |

Then we heard voices, coming from somewhere beyond the bushes. Two boys appeared, followed by an older man. They greeted us, grinning. In fact, they might have been laughing at us. We didn't care. Greetings were

exchanged. People are very polite in Malawi.

| 41 | |

We left the car on and followed them down a series of dark winding tracks, without knowing who they were or where they were taking us. At last we came to a small hamlet, half a dozen thatched mud-walled houses, all closed up for the night. They called, and a man emerged from one of the houses; he was tall, and blind in one eye. We asked whether we could stay at the Maia Beach accommodation. Apparently unsurprised by these three pale strangers who'd turned up on his doorstep in the middle of the night, he smiled his assent. He fetched keys, and we followed him as he set off again down a winding track through the bushes.

| 42 | |

And there, along the shore, was a cluster of small bamboo huts. One was opened up for us. A torch was found. A price was agreed. Bedding was brought. The mosquito nets were full of holes, but I had a sewing kit, and the kindness of our hosts more than made up for any discomforts.

| 43 | |

The next morning we were woken by bright sunlight, needling through the cracks in the bamboo wall, and the sound of children's voices. I pushed open the door of our hut, and gasped at the sheer beauty of our surroundings. We'd landed in paradise. There, just a few metres away, was a crescent of silver sand lapped by the crystal water of the lake. A couple of palm trees waved lazy branches against the sun. A gaggle of ragged smiling children had gathered at our door, chattering excitedly. As I stepped outside, they fell silent for a moment, then burst into a chorus: 'Good afternoon. Good morning. How are you? Do you speak English? What is your name?'

A It didn't take many words to explain what had happened. With some careful manoeuvering and some brute force, slowly, slowly, we inched on to firmer ground. We asked for directions to the Maia Beach resort. It transpired that it had closed down last year but someone in a nearby village had a key.

B It was that dangerous time when the roads are swarming with villagers and their animals, and drivers of vehicles without functioning lights or brakes career around potholes, also hurrying homewards. For twilight is short in Malawi, and when night comes, the darkness is absolute.

C After a while they thinned out and I could see the soft star-lit glimmer of Lake Malawi spread before us like a wide swathe of grey silk, so still you'd never have guessed it was water, apart from a faint ripple that wrinkled its surface when the breeze stirred.

D We drove back slowly, seeking a turning off the road, a track towards the lake, but there was no opening, not even a gap between the prickly bushes where the track should have been, only the same unremitting vista of low trees, bushes and sand.

E This place, we were told, had been created by an English couple who intended to use the proceeds to fund a school and a health centre in the village. But few tourists had ever made it here, and no one knew whether the couple would ever return.

F Suddenly, out of the dusk, a crooked, hand-painted wooden sign flickered across our headlights: 'Maia Beach Cafe Accommodation'. We let out a cheer, executed a U-turn, and set out down the sandy track signposted towards the beach.

G We held our breath and listened to the silence. Somewhere far away there was a sound of drumming, and we could smell wood smoke, which suggested some kind of habitation.

H Then, all of a sudden, our wheels hit a patch of soft sand, skidded, and sank in. Getting out to assess the situation, we saw that three wheels were hopelessly churning up the sand; the fourth was spinning free, perched over a sandy bluff with a four-foot drop beneath. If we slipped down there, we would never, ever get the car out again.

Part 7

You are going to read extracts from an article about favourite old songs. For questions **44–53**, choose from the sections (**A–E**). The extracts may be chosen more than once. Mark your answers **on the separate answer sheet.**

Which extract mentions

the possibility of varying interpretations of this version of the song?

44	

the technical limitations of the musician?

45	

an example of the artist adopting a particular identity?

46	

awareness of self-delusion?

47	

a restored reputation?

48	

the increased personal significance that a song has come to have?

49	

some thoughts on the nature of hero worship?

50	

a suggestion that all is not lost?

51	

the ability of music to evoke the past?

52	

an instance of personal satisfaction?

53	

Old Music

Five people write about musicians and songs that have been important to them in their life

A

At Last I Am Free by Robert Wyatt

Originally written for those masters of disco, Chic, it seems a long journey to Robert Wyatt's version. Wyatt is one of the great heroes of British counter-culture, whose blend of political commitment and musical experiment has led to a career of almost unrivalled range and influence. On this song he combines the heartbreaking honesty familiar from his other work with a voice that is somehow at once shrill but deeply soulful and communicative. The lyrics speak of a failing relationship but the way Wyatt sings it could be about anything – any momentous parting or new beginnings. The line 'I can hardly see in front of me' is one of those phrases in pop music that come along from time to time that mean almost nothing yet bulge under the weight of a thousand projected meanings for a thousand different listeners.

B

Another Day by Roy Harper

Decades on from its 1974 release 'Another Day' still strikes me as one of the most poignant and beautiful songs ever; a regretful ode to a lost love encountered once again, full of thwarted possibilities that the singer acknowledges but refuses to grasp and with regrets on both sides about things that should have been said but were not. At the song's end, even the possibility for words runs out as the former lovers stand with the shades of their former selves awkwardly between them. Others have covered the song, but none is better than Harper's original version, which Harper himself believes to be one of the 'best love songs I wrote'. Although Harper's beautiful, angry and sometimes passionate songs fell into a quiet obscurity for a while, these days he is namechecked at almost every turn by modern-day artists.

C

Say Hello Wave Goodbye by Soft Cell

This song is a time machine for men and women of a certain age. Soft Cell had questionable credibility even then, so this was always a guilty pleasure for me. It has one of the best opening lines, ever – 'I never went to the Pink Flamingo, but if I had, I am sure I would have found someone in the doorway, crying in the rain'. It was all slightly seedy – a down-at-heel, defeated romanticism. The oboe hitting the high notes offers a sharp reminder that singer Marc Almond can't manage the same, but the combination of the two works a treat, backed by a rhythm that doesn't seem to want to end. Back then, the pain was all imagined. Thirty years on, you can wallow in proper melancholy all you like. But make sure the kids are out.

D

Maggie May by Rod Stewart

I once went to an 18th birthday party disco. 'Maggie May' came on and instantly the place erupted; at least half a dozen strapping blokes more suited to the great outdoors started marching around clutching invisible microphone stands. It was a bizarre sight, but testimony to the hold that Stewart had at that time over lads who felt compelled to ape him. What is it about that song? A mood of end-of-summer rueful regret, mingled with rite of passage reminiscence? It came out in September 1971; I had just broken up with a girl who was admittedly nothing like woman-of-the-world Maggie. But 'you made a first-class fool out of me' – well, I kidded myself that rang true, at the time. Perhaps it was just the footballs, scarves, and glorious, ramshackle live appearances that appealed to men my age.

E

Martha by Tom Waits

Written when Tom Waits was just 24, 'Martha' finds this earliest incarnation of one of the US's most intriguing musical characters dropping comfortably into the slippers of a much, much older man. Calling long-distance to an old flame, he lays his heart bare about their past together and offers the beautifully underplayed revelation that he is still in love with her. The poignancy of this call taking place when both are probably now well into their 50s is given added weight – that so much time could never erase this strength of feeling. The lyrics make you wish you could be there to see these two fictional characters reunited. In the age of social media, this track stands as a memorial to a time when you could easily lose touch with someone so very close to you, as time marched brutally on.

WRITING (1 hour 30 minutes)

Part 1

Read the two texts below.

Write an essay summarising and evaluating the key points from both texts. Use your own words throughout as far as possible, and include your own ideas in your answers.

Write your answer in **240–280** words.

1

Dress and Image

When professionals such as bank managers or lawyers wear formal clothes, they are often sending out a clear signal that they wish to maintain a degree of distance and detachment from those they serve. Their style of dress suggests that the atmosphere is unlikely to be light-hearted or relaxed. In fact, there is no doubt that many of us would be somewhat uncomfortable if we walked into the office of a bank manager or lawyer who was dressed casually. Somehow, formal clothes communicate the message 'I am competent and you can trust me', and naturally we feel reassured by this.

The Impact of Dress

Many jobs involve wearing a uniform but the authority this suggests can be intimidating to some people who may instinctively feel that they are put at a disadvantage. For some purposes therefore, such as when police have to deal with particularly vulnerable people, informal clothes may be more appropriate. Of course, there are some important public occasions, such as coronations and state funerals, for which the wearing of elaborate formal dress is an integral part of the ceremony; it might be deemed disrespectful if this critical custom were not observed.

Write your **essay**.

Part 2

Write an answer to **one** of the questions 2–5 in this part. Write your answer in **280–320** words in an appropriate style.

2 An English language magazine is running a series on the topic of happiness. You decide to send in an article. You should briefly describe one or two situations in which you have experienced a sense of happiness. You should also analyse what contributes to feelings of happiness for many people, and suggest whether the pursuit of happiness is a worthwhile aim.

Write your **article**.

3 A cultural magazine is planning a series on historical exhibitions organised by museums that have captured the imagination of the public. You decide to submit a review of an exhibition with a historical theme that has impressed you. Your review should briefly describe the exhibition, explain why you think it was successful, and assess the importance of such exhibitions in educating the public about history.

Write your **review**.

4 An international newspaper is inviting readers to contribute letters on the topic of speakers who have inspired them. You decide to write a letter about a speaker you heard recently. You should explain what was particularly inspiring about this speaker and assess the value of listening to inspirational speakers in general.

Write your **letter**.

5 Write an answer to **one** of the following two questions based on **one** of the titles below. Write **5(a)** or **5(b)** at the beginning of your answer.

(a) Chinua Achebe: *Things Fall Apart*
Members of your reading group have been asked to review books which deal with the theme of justice in different societies. You decide to write a review of *Things Fall Apart*. Your review should briefly consider the approach to justice taken by Okonkwo's clan and assess the impact that approach has on people's lives.

Write your **review**.

(b) J.B. Priestley: *An Inspector Calls*
As a member of your college drama group you have been asked to write a report for the group in preparation for their production of *An Inspector Calls*. Your report should briefly describe the ways in which the Birling family respond to the Inspector's questions, and how the attitudes of Mr. and Mrs. Birling contrast with those of their children.

Write your **report**.

LISTENING (40 minutes approximately)

Part 1

You will hear three different extracts.

For questions **1–6**, choose the answer (**A**, **B** or **C**) which fits best according to what you hear.

There are two questions for each extract.

Extract One

You hear a woman talking on the radio about a small mammal called the hedgehog.

1 What is her attitude to the reduction in the number of hedgehogs in Britain?

   A She is concerned at the part played by cats.
   B She is disinclined to take it very seriously.
   C She thinks it may affect other animals.

2 What does she suggest about threats to wildlife?

   A Some species are more important than others.
   B Politicians are too slow in taking action.
   C There are more pressing priorities.

Extract Two

You hear an entrepreneur called Patrick Schwerdtfeger giving a talk at a business conference.

3 Patrick uses the example of a skyscraper

   A to emphasise how competitive people need to be.
   B to illustrate that anything is possible with determination.
   C to show that you need imagination to succeed.

4 Patrick thinks that 'realistic' goals

   A display a lack of ambition.
   B may offer little sense of achievement.
   C can be too popular.

Extract Three

You hear part of an interview with a man called Maurice Parks, who owns a small independent publishing company.

5 Maurice feels his professional approach is unusual because

    A   he does not make assumptions about authors.
    B   he is more selective than traditional publishers.
    C   he does not believe in rushing the editing process.

6 Maurice says editors in big publishing companies are driven by

    A   the search for new formats.
    B   the need to create profits.
    C   the safeguarding of their reputation.

Part 2

You will hear a radio presenter called Tom Lee describing the psychological effects of the colour red on humans and animals.

For questions **7–15**, complete the sentences with a word or short phrase.

Psychologists at a British university found those taking part in
(7) .... competitions got more points when they wore red.

Tom says it is becoming increasingly clear that colours affect how the human
(8) .... behaves.

Anthropologist Ella Beecham identified a possible **(9)** .... when she discovered how colours were assigned in some Olympic events.

Beecham found wearing red affected results most when wrestlers were what is referred to as
(10) ....

Beecham believes that unexpected results may occur when a
(11) .... has an unconscious preference for red.

Beecham investigated whether different levels of **(12)** .... had a favourable effect on those playing in the same team.

Tom uses the words **(13)** .... and
.... to describe the meaning that red often has in nature.

Fish in an aquarium behaved in a way normally reserved for encounters with
(14) .... when a red vehicle was nearby.

In mandrill monkeys, red signifies the **(15)** .... of the male in cases of possible conflict.

Part 3

You will hear a radio programme in which two people, Alison Kreel and David Walsh, who each run a food business, are discussing the premises they share.

For questions **16–20**, choose the answer (**A**, **B**, **C** or **D**) which fits best according to what you hear.

16   Alison and David agree that the market for quality food products

   A   is experiencing greater growth than ever.
   B   is becoming increasingly sophisticated.
   C   has a thirst for constant innovation.
   D   can only thrive in particular locations.

17   David thinks that the Siston building attracted funding easily because

   A   it was considered the best way to start regenerating a run-down industrial area.
   B   it was less risky than financing individual entrepreneurs.
   C   it was thought it would give new food companies valuable support.
   D   it was part of a drive to increase local employment opportunities.

18   They both agree the main benefit of using a shared kitchen space is cost savings and

   A   being able to get advice from fellow entrepreneurs.
   B   being able to share marketing opportunities.
   C   having a supportive working environment.
   D   having access to top-of-the-range equipment and facilities.

19   How has Alison's vision for her business changed since moving into the Siston building?

   A   She has realised that she needs to expand her range of products.
   B   She now sees that opening a shop and café would have been too risky.
   C   She has decided she prefers the idea of selling to small local businesses.
   D   She no longer thinks becoming a nationally recognised brand is achievable.

20   What advice would Alison and David give to any aspiring entrepreneur?

   A   Work out costs carefully.
   B   Don't spend too much time planning.
   C   Get some relevant work experience.
   D   Don't waste time on low margin products.

Part 4

You will hear five short extracts in which people talk about studying abroad.

TASK ONE

For questions **21–25**, choose from the list (**A–H**) the reason each speaker gives for wanting to study abroad.

TASK TWO

For questions **26–30**, choose from the list (**A–H**) how each speaker felt about their studies abroad.

While you listen, you must complete both tasks.

TASK ONE		TASK TWO	
A to experience another culture		**A** reassured by the available support facilities	
B to improve foreign language competence		**B** concerned about the high tuition fees	
C to improve job prospects	Speaker 1 [ ] 21	**C** impressed with the international nature of the institution	Speaker 1 [ ] 26
D to get a different perspective on a subject	Speaker 2 [ ] 22	**D** surprised by the contrast with undergraduate study	Speaker 2 [ ] 27
E to experience a different teaching method	Speaker 3 [ ] 23	**E** disappointed by the academic standards	Speaker 3 [ ] 28
F to make useful contacts	Speaker 4 [ ] 24	**F** satisfied with the accommodation	Speaker 4 [ ] 29
G to become more independent	Speaker 5 [ ] 25	**G** pleased to find the learning goals achievable	Speaker 5 [ ] 30
H to live closer to extended family		**H** challenged by the amount of self study	

SPEAKING (16 minutes)

There are two examiners. One (the interlocutor) conducts the test, providing you with the necessary materials and explaining what you have to do. The other examiner (the assessor) will be introduced to you, but then takes no further part in the interaction.

Part 1 (2 minutes)

The interlocutor first asks you and your partner a few questions which focus on information about yourselves.

Part 2 (4 minutes)

In this part of the test you and your partner are asked to talk together. The interlocutor places a set of pictures on the table in front of you. There may be only one picture in the set or as many as seven pictures. This stimulus provides the basis for a discussion. The interlocutor first asks an introductory question which focuses on two of the pictures (or in the case of a single picture, on aspects of the picture). After about a minute, the interlocutor gives you both a decision-making task based on the same set of pictures.

The pictures for Part 2 are on page C4 of the colour section.

Part 3 (10 minutes)

You are each given the opportunity to talk for two minutes, to comment after your partner has spoken and to take part in a more general discussion.

The interlocutor gives you a card with a question written on it and asks you to talk about it for two minutes. After you have spoken, the interlocutor asks you both another question related to the topic on the card, addressing your partner first. This procedure is repeated, so that your partner receives a card and speaks for two minutes and a follow-up question is asked.

Finally, the interlocutor asks some further questions, which lead to a discussion on a general theme related to the subjects already covered in Part 3.

The cards for Part 3 are on pages C6–C7 of the colour section.

Test 4

READING AND USE OF ENGLISH (1 hour 30 minutes)

Part 1

For questions **1–8**, read the text below and decide which answer (**A**, **B**, **C** or **D**) best fits each gap.

Mark your answers **on the separate answer sheet**.

There is an example at the beginning (**0**).

| **0** | **A** | lingering | **B** | enduring | **C** | unceasing | **D** | perennial |

0	A	B	C	D

The importance of saving plastic

Many artefacts of (**0**) ……..... cultural significance from the last century were made from plastic. It was always confidently assumed that this rather (**1**) ……..... material was virtually indestructible. Now that some of these artefacts have become museum (**2**) ……....., we have discovered that this (**3**) ……..... was sadly mistaken.

The degradation of plastics is worrying both scientists and historians, who are racing against time to save our plastic heritage before it (**4**) ……..... into dust. Our love affair with plastics (**5**) ……..... in large part from the fact they can be moulded into just about any shape imaginable. When it comes to longevity, however, they have a serious (**6**) ……....: their chemical structure breaks down when they are exposed to air and sunlight.

Many now argue that we must consider the cultural (**7**) ……..... we will be leaving future generations. Without urgent (**8**) ……..... many artefacts will be lost forever. But developing effective conservation strategies is difficult because what works to preserve one type of plastic can have a catastrophic effect on the lifespan of another.

1 **A** trivial   **B** routine   **C** customary   **D** mundane

2 **A** items   **B** articles   **C** pieces   **D** objects

3 **A** concept   **B** premise   **C** notion   **D** proposition

4 **A** crumbles   **B** shatters   **C** erodes   **D** shrivels

5 **A** starts   **B** sparks   **C** stems   **D** sprouts

6 **A** fault   **B** snag   **C** stigma   **D** flaw

7 **A** bequest   **B** legacy   **C** endowment   **D** heirloom

8 **A** intervention   **B** interception   **C** interference   **D** intercession

Part 2

For questions **9–16**, read the text below and think of the word which best fits each space. Use only one word in each space. There is an example at the beginning (**0**). Write your answers **IN CAPITAL LETTERS on the separate answer sheet.**

Example: | **0** | *O* | N | | | | | | | | | | | | | | | | | |

Is nothing impossible?

It is certainly the case that believers in 'nothing is impossible' base their blind optimism

(0) ……….. a kernel of truth. Strictly **(9)** ………., as logicians are keen to remind us, only

(10) ………. which involves a logical contradiction is impossible. So two plus two cannot equal

five, **(11)** ………. can there ever be any truly square circles. However, the limits that most of us

have in **(12)** ………. when we worry about our lives are rarely logical.

For as **(13)** ………. as something remains logically possible, some people can't help

(14) ………. wonder if their dream might become reality. This is exacerbated by the fact that

our culture encourages people to **(15)** ………. big and believe that 'impossibility' is nothing more

than the creation of a negative mind.

It is far simpler, though, to concentrate on levels of difficulty and chances of success. If the former

are too high and the latter too low, there's hardly any point in adding 'but it isn't impossible,

(16) ………. enough desire or support'.

Part 3

For questions **17–24**, read the text below. Use the word given in capitals at the end of some of the lines to form a word that fits in the space in the same line. There is an example at the beginning (**0**). Write your answers **IN CAPITAL LETTERS on the separate answer sheet**.

Example:

| 0 | U | N | P | R | E | C | E | D | E | N | T | E | D | | | | |

Living in a digital age

Today, our life is filled with noise, words and images to an (**0**) .... degree,   **PRECEDE**

with people spending much of their time connected to different forms of

media. Consider the 'quiet carriage' signs found on many UK trains; these are

indications that passengers must be (**17**) .... requested to refrain from   **SPECIFY**

talking on their mobile phones.

The greatest advantages of wired living are easily (**18**) .... Plugged into   **NUMERATE**

the web, we can research and (**19**) .... much of humanity's gathered   **REFER**

knowledge – in minutes. We have almost (**20**) .... capabilities, and we   **IMAGINE**

are becoming increasingly adept at using them. When we are unplugged,

we can demonstrate the capacity to make decisions and to act on our own

(**21**) .... We therefore need to appreciate the value of being able to   **INITIATE**

function both online and offline. However (**22**) .... technology becomes   **PERVADE**

in the future, we need to think (**23**) .... and to learn how to assess its   **CRITIC**

(**24**) .... as well as its advantages in order to make discerning use of   **COMING**

it in our lives.

Part 4

For questions **25–30**, complete the second sentence so that it has a similar meaning to the first sentence, using the word given. **Do not change the word given**. You must use between **three** and **eight** words, including the word given. Here is an example (**0**).

Example:

0 Do you mind if I watch you while you paint?

objection

Do you .... you while you paint?

0	have any objection to my watching

Write **only** the missing words **on the separate answer sheet**.

---

25   How likely is it that Tom will get a place in the team?

chances

What .... getting a place in the team?

26   It has never been explained why he decided to relinquish his position as director.

decision

No .... to relinquish his position as director.

27   Sam doesn't think he'll be able to come with us at the weekend.

prospect

Sam sees .... to come with us at the weekend.

28 Harry has worked hard but it remains to be seen whether he'll win the prize.

time

Harry has worked hard but .... whether he'll win the prize.

29 Luigi decided not to bring up the subject of his salary at the first meeting.

no

Luigi decided to .... the subject of his salary at the first meeting.

30 The professor said that, as far as he knows, the results of the research are accurate.

best

The professor said that .... the results of the research are accurate.

Part 5

You are going to read a magazine article about graphic novels. For questions **31–36**, choose the answer (**A**, **B**, **C** or **D**) which you think fits best according to the text. Mark your answers **on the separate answer sheet**.

Graphic novels: a fresh angle on literature

*Has the graphic novel – a fictional story presented in comic-strip format –
finally become intellectually respectable?*

Graphic novels have just landed with an almighty *kersplat*. Ten days ago, two such works were shortlisted for the Shakespeare Book Awards for the first time in the history of the prize, in two different categories. This was no publicity stunt: neither panel knew what the other had done. This is, surely, the moment when the graphic book finally made its entrance into the respectable club room of high literature. Hang on, though: can you compare a graphic novel with the literary kind? Wouldn't that be like comparing a painting with a music video? Or is it time we started seeing them as comparable mediums for storytelling? If so, what next?

Robert Macfarlane, the chairman of another major literary award, says he has no objection in principle to a graphic novel being submitted for the prize. In fact, he has taught one, Art Spiegelman's *Maus*, alongside the works of Russian writer Tolstoy and *Don Quixote* (by the Spanish writer Miguel de Cervantes) at the University of Cambridge, where he works in the English Faculty. 'The idea of outlawing the graphic novel doesn't make any sense to me,' he says. 'I don't segregate it from the novel. The novel is always eating up other languages, media and forms.' Graphic fiction, he says, is 'another version of the novel's long flirtation with the visual'. This is, he declares, 'a golden age for the graphic novel'.

And he's right. We are seeing a boom in graphic novels. Since *Maus* was awarded a Pulitzer Prize in 1992, they have gone on to devour every literary genre going. But so far, graphic novels have politely stood aside and let conventional books win the big prizes. Now they want the vote. Fighting for the graphic novelists' cause, astonishingly, are some hefty prize-winning writers. The English novelist and poet A. S. Byatt is passionately in favour of graphic novels competing with regular ones. Byatt, who is a huge fan of Spiegelman's *Maus*, thinks that French-Iranian artist Marjane Satrapi's graphic novel *Persepolis* stands 'head and shoulders above most novels being produced. It's more interesting and more moving. It's able to be serious because it can carry itself along on this unserious form. It allowed her to be witty about things that are terrible. And that's why it's a major work of art'.

The genius of the graphic novel, as the English writer Philip Pullman explains, is that it can bring into play so many levels of narrative by layering them on top of each other. Take American Alison Bechdel's brilliant *Are You My Mother?* – in a single page, she can depict a memory of being with her mother in her childhood, dialogue between herself and her mother as they chat on the phone in the present, plus an image of herself toiling at her desk, trying to write her memoir. And what Bechdel and her mum are saying on the phone links to the diaries of the early 20th-century writer Virginia Woolf, which Bechdel also brings to visual life. Try doing that with words – it would take a chapter. Bechdel does it in a few panels. That, in the end, is precisely what keeps graphic literature so distinct from prose narrative.

Graphic novels and traditional novels demand, to be sure, the same amounts of time, intellect and artistry from their authors. But that doesn't mean they're the same thing. A few years on, will you be clicking the buy button on a graphic novel as happily as you'd pick up a work by a traditional novelist? Even Bechdel confesses that her reading habits are still struggling out of the past. 'Honestly, I would be slightly more inclined to pick up a non-graphic work,' she says. 'At this point, there's not a huge number of graphic novels that are about topics that interest me. But that, too, is changing. We're becoming more visually literate. There's some reason for these graphic novels creeping into the canon. We're reading differently from how we used to 200 years ago.'

31 What does the writer say about the nomination of two graphic novels for the Shakespeare Book Awards?

   A It revealed the closed-mindedness of the literary establishment.
   B It was a result of confusion among members of the panel.
   C It generated debate about the true purpose of the prize.
   D It was not deliberately calculated to attract people's attention.

32 What does Robert Macfarlane suggest about graphic novels?

   A Their long-term success has now been assured.
   B Their banning from literature courses has backfired.
   C They are a logical step in the development of fiction.
   D They tend to be less innovative than traditional novels.

33 In the third paragraph, the writer suggests that, in the past, writers of graphic novels

   A lacked the support of influential figures.
   B were systematically discriminated against.
   C tended to accept their inferior social standing.
   D underappreciated the importance of literary awards.

34 The writer discusses Alison Bechdel's book to make the point that graphic novels

   A can have just as much narrative depth as traditional novels.
   B are able to incorporate a surprising range of different voices.
   C can represent the workings of memory in sophisticated ways.
   D enable writers to deal with different aspects of a story at once.

35 Bechdel is quoted in the last paragraph to make the point that

   A interest in graphic novels reflects a more general trend.
   B many readers lack the skills to fully appreciate graphic novels.
   C it is difficult to persuade people to take graphic novels seriously.
   D graphic novels are far outnumbered by quality traditional novels.

36 In this article, the writer is

   A analysing the preoccupations of graphic novelists.
   B outlining the origins of graphic novels.
   C describing the working practices of graphic novelists.
   D evaluating the merits of graphic novels.

Part 6

You are going to read an article about London Zoo. Seven paragraphs have been removed from the extract. Choose from the paragraphs **A–H** the one which fits each gap (**37–43**). There is one extra paragraph which you do not need to use. Mark your answers **on the separate answer sheet**.

London Zoo's new Tiger Territory

London Zoo, one of the oldest in the world, is an architectural jumble. Has its £3.6m Tiger Territory put things right?

'We have tried our best to fade into the background,' says Michael Kozdon, architect of the new £3.6m Tiger Territory at London Zoo. It's not often you hear an architect say that, but then it's not often you have a pair of endangered Sumatran tigers called Jae Jae and Melati as clients, either. 'In the past,' continues Kozdon, 'animal enclosures were all about creating an iconic architectural statement. Now the emphasis is on animal welfare, on bringing visitors as close to the creatures as possible. Our aim is to disappear.'

37	

The enclosure's sinuous silhouette echoes the pinkish peaks of its neighbour, the Mappin Terraces, a man-made range of rocky mountains that have long poked their summits above the trees, bringing a surreal air to this strange corner of the park. Built in 1914, this elevated landscape was the result of a clause governing the zoo's expansion: an additional land grab of four acres would only be allowed if the animals they housed could be visible from the rest of the park. Sadly, this sheer geological formation, erupting above the neat neoclassical terraces of north west London, has been barren since 1985, when Pipaluk, the last of the polar bears, was finally moved out after 18 years.

38	

'Tigers are avid climbers,' explains Robin Fitzgerald, the zoo's project manager. 'They like to observe their terrain from a towering vantage point, so we've given them a habitat that lets them do exactly that – with a view out over Regent's Park.' Describing how the poles and canopy support each other, he adds: 'It's basically circus tent technology.' Neatly complying with the brief to all but vanish into thin air, this means there is no need for the extra steel structures that are so common in the zoo's other mesh enclosures – such as Cedric Price's famous Snowdon Aviary.

39	

The former now provides a cosy den for the tigers, complete with heated rocks to soothe their weary muscles, while the latter has become an elevated area for visitors, with panoramic windows looking out across the Indonesian-inspired landscaping of the enclosure. From here, you can watch the tigers happily splashing about in their pool, or scaling the feeding poles to devour chicken wings and steak.

40	

Such practical details are a far cry from many of the zoo's more famous structures, most of which were designed to maximise exotic spectacle. Founded in 1828 as the world's first scientific zoological gardens, the site has become burdened by the weight of its own history. From the start, when it was laid out by Decimus Burton, the zoo employed architects of the highest calibre – leaving it with a legacy of protected buildings.

41	

Next door to the Tiger Territory are the bulbous flanks of the majestic elephant and rhinoceros pavilion, designed by Hugh Casson in 1965 to evoke a herd of elephants gathered around a watering hole, their huge rumps jostling for position. Topped with triangular roof lights intended to call to mind nodding heads and swinging trunks, the pavilion was commissioned 'to display these animals in the most dramatic way'.

42	

The unavoidable strategy of make-do-and-mend renders London Zoo an inevitably dated institution, laden with rigid monuments conceived in another era that it must now either work with or around building design safari as a wildlife one. Victorian kiosks jostle uncomfortably with mock Tudor clocktowers; lichen-encrusted steel spaceframes cantilever out over brutalist concrete terraces.

43	

London Zoo is a fascinating piece of living heritage. With its vastly increased area, near-invisible structure, and strategic re-use of what is already there, the Tiger Territory points a promising way forward. 'The challenge is far greater than it used to be,' says Kozdon. 'Before, architecture led the way. Now the best situation would be to have no buildings at all.'

A However, the Tiger Territory had other constraints to grapple with. With a limited area of 36 acres in one of London's most protected settings, the zoo was forced to modify what it had – in this case, a Victorian stork and ostrich house and a 1960s sea lion viewing platform, both of which had been off-limits to visitors for 30 years.

B But this heritage is a mixed blessing. Take the 1934 penguin pool, a sleek and slender double helix of ramping concrete floating above a blue oval pool. Faces tend to fall when visitors find it empty – the bright white surfaces apparently damaged the penguins' eyes, and the concrete was too hard on their feet. It now stands as an unused but still-loved relic of a bygone age.

C This explains its importance as an important breeding centre for tigers. Tiger Territory's two Sumatran tigers are the most genetically important pair of tigers in Europe. With high hopes for breeding resting on the pair, their cubs would be the first to be born at the zoo for more than 15 years.

D A look inside is telling: the space for visitors far exceeds the narrow nooks created for the immense creatures. The vast structure is now home to bearded pigs and pygmy hippos – tubby, low-slung creatures that seem out of place in the building's soaring, top-lit reaches.

E This architectural jumble all comes to a strange climax in the stripped classical facade of the 1920s aquarium, with its arched entranceway and symmetrical windows now squeezed beneath the colossal mock-rocks of what was once Bear Mountain – itself used to house tanks of water for the fish below.

F This explains why, rather than being held in by a roof, the animals have a fine net canopy stretching above their heads – even though its silken threads are made of 3 mm steel cable. The canopy soars above the treetops of Regent's Park like a giant spider's web.

G Thanks to the Tiger Territory, the skyline of the zoo is now newly populated. The new enclosure boasts several mature plane trees, as well as tall wooden feeding poles fitted with pulleys that hoist big chunks of meat aloft. So, before they can sink their three-inch teeth into lunch, the animals will first have to go up them, which suits their predatory nature.

H These design features demonstrate a new emphasis on animal welfare. This extends to the pairing of the animals, which was meticulously planned. But if needed, the pair can be separated, along with any future cubs, into two different parts of the enclosure, connected by a glass door.

Part 7

You are going to read extracts from an introduction to a book about the study of children. For questions **44–53**, choose from the sections (**A–E**). The sections may be chosen more than once. Mark your answers **on the separate answer sheet**.

In which section are the following mentioned?

the need to be aware of bias in interpretation	**44** ☐
the lack of documentation on certain children	**45** ☐
the lack of consensus regarding children's capabilities	**46** ☐
sources of misleading views on children	**47** ☐
the interdependence of different approaches to studying childhood	**48** ☐
a concern about the implication of differences in maturity between children	**49** ☐
a case for recognising exceptions to traditional characteristics	**50** ☐
valuing children's opinions in current debates	**51** ☐
how laws have come to define a child	**52** ☐
the proportion of children in certain societies	**53** ☐

Understanding childhood

A

Common sense suggests a child is someone who is young, who is smaller, more immature and vulnerable and in many other ways different to human adults. The pioneer anthropologist of childhood Margaret Mead believed children everywhere were 'pygmies among giants, ignorant among the knowledgeable, wordless among the inarticulate'. Half a century later, there is good reason to challenge this universal prescription for young humanity. Children share in common that they are growing, changing and learning, but they differ in innumerable ways in the expression of growth and change, as well as in the circumstances, goals and extent of their learning. They are not universally seen as weak, wordless or ignorant. Childhood is viewed very differently depending on the geographical area under investigation and the period of time under study as well as the standpoint of the person studying it.

B

This book is as much about studying the cultural beliefs, representations and discourses of childhood as about studying children's physical and psychological immaturity, growth and development. Of course, the two are linked. Key questions are raised about children – their needs, competences, responsibilities and rights. Put simply, how far are they seen as innocents who need protection, nurture and training, and how far as social actors who engage with and contribute to their development, and who have a right to be heard? The near universal adoption of the United Nations Convention on the Rights of the Child has come to symbolize a profound and challenging shift in perspective, especially its emphasis on children's participatory rights. This is reflected in the way this book includes perspectives of children and young people on many of the issues being discussed.

C

The United Nations Convention on the Rights of the Child perceives a child to be anyone under the age of eighteen, which is also consistent with much national and international legislation. But what does this vast cross-section of the world's population – in some countries nearly half the population – have in common that justifies a single formal designation? This is not just an issue of diversity between societies. It is also about the varieties of childhood within the broad age span nought to eighteen years. The child of five months is worlds apart from the child of five years, as is the five year old from the fifteen year old. In many ways, a fifteen-year-old 'child' has more in common with a twenty-five-year-old 'adult' than with a five-year-old 'child'.

D

Developmental psychology has provided detailed descriptions of the many stages and transitions that take place within Western childhoods, which are also reflected in everyday distinctions in the English language – for example, between babies, toddlers, school children, teenagers and young people. Distinguishing kinds of childhood by finely divided ages is not universal. In some societies, children's ages have not always been recorded; their status has been determined by their abilities, their social class or caste and their gender, not by their age. Defining childhood as a distinctive life phase is also premised on assumptions about adulthood. There is good reason to challenge the contrast between the dependent, vulnerable, developing child and the autonomous, mature, knowing adult – for example, by acknowledging situations where adults may be vulnerable and children may be resilient.

E

A guiding principle in planning this book has been to acknowledge wherever possible that knowledge, beliefs and understanding about childhood are culturally situated. Much scientific research on childhood, especially in developmental psychology, has been criticized for presenting its conclusions as universal truths, even though the research was based on children and young people growing up in industrialized societies, especially in Europe and North America. In the same way, dominant discourses of childhood innocence have to be understood in the context of Western history and cultural traditions. This issue applies even more strongly in relation to the study of children's rights, where one of the key debates is about how far the United Nations Convention on the Rights of the Child projects a universalized image of the individualized child which fails to take account of competing cultural traditions.

WRITING (1 hour 30 minutes)

Part 1

Read the two texts below.

Write an essay summarising and evaluating the key points from both texts. Use your own words throughout as far as possible, and include your own ideas in your answers.

Write your answer in **240–280** words.

1
Looking back

Memories are undoubtedly precious to all of us. We can get a huge amount of pleasure and reassurance from the simple act of sitting down with relatives or friends and reminiscing about past events, whether they are amusing incidents from our childhood, teenage adventures or turning points in our lives. Given this, it has to be said that we should be suspicious of any tendency in ourselves or others to fall into the trap of constantly comparing the present with the past. Surely it is better to be focused entirely on the here and now?

Remembering how it was

Memories are more than merely a source of delight; on a more profound level they contribute to our sense of identity. All the experiences we have had make us the people we are today, and without our unique set of memories we would be utterly different. It should not be overlooked that memories can also be unreliable and inconsistent. After all, as the police are well aware, two or three witnesses will often remember the same event in ways that flatly contradict one another. Even close relatives such as siblings will usually have strikingly different memories of a shared family holiday.

Write your **essay**.

Part 2

Write an answer to **one** of the questions **2–5** in this part. Write your answer in **280–320** words in an appropriate style.

2 An international newspaper has asked for articles from readers on the theme 'Small World'. You decide to write an article. You should briefly describe some of the effects of global developments in communications, such as travel and social networking. You should also evaluate how the consequences of these developments may affect your own country's cultural identity.

Write your **article**.

3 You are the leader of a local youth group. You have been asked to write a report for your local website on social activities available for young people in your area. In your report you should explain how two or three activities available locally help young people to interact socially. You should also assess the importance of social life in the personal development of young people.

Write your **report**.

4 You recently attended a jobs fair organised for students in their final year at university by a number of major international companies. You decide to write a review of the event for your student newspaper. You should briefly describe one or two jobs which attracted you. Your review should also evaluate how well different companies marketed themselves at the jobs fair in order to attract potential employees.

Write your **review**.

5 Write an answer to **one** of the following two questions based on **one** of the titles below. Write **5(a)** or **5(b)** at the beginning of your answer

(a)   John Wyndham: *The Day of the Triffids*
In your literature class you have been discussing the ways in which writers portray characters in their novels. Your tutor has asked you to write an essay comparing the characters of Bill and Josella, and assessing how they come to terms with the difficulties they encounter.

Write your **essay**.

(b)   L. P. Hartley: *The Go-Between*
A literary journal has published an article on 'novels with the loss of innocence as a central theme'. It has invited readers to send in letters recommending examples of such novels. You decide to recommend *The Go-Between*. You should briefly describe the story and explain why you think the theme of lost innocence is central to the novel.

Write your **letter.**

LISTENING (40 minutes approximately)

Part 1

You will hear three different extracts.

For questions **1–6**, choose the answer (**A**, **B** or **C**) which fits best according to what you hear.

There are two questions for each extract.

Extract One

You hear one of the owners of a tea supplier in the UK talking on the radio about his business.

1 The man mentions a few clicks of a mouse in order to emphasise that

    A   the company's website has been designed with ease of use in mind.
    B   the company makes no attempt to conceal its connections.
    C   the company's critics have not carried out basic research.

2 What is he doing when he speaks?

    A   stressing the company's lack of reliance on its backers
    B   describing the backers' attempts to influence the company
    C   predicting a reduced role for the backers in future

Extract Two

You hear an academic called Carl Miller talking about playing games.

3 Carl makes a comparison between games and systems in order to suggest how games

    A   help people to cope with the modern world.
    B   encourage people to be more competitive.
    C   reduce people's appreciation of true culture.

4 What is Carl doing when he talks about board games?

    A   justifying his enjoyment of digital media
    B   suggesting that humans are inherently social
    C   emphasising the value of their link to the past

Extract Three

You hear a business presenter called Bill Craven talking about human behaviour.

5 What aspect of great leaders and organisations is Bill focusing on?

   A the techniques by which they achieve uniformity
   B their ability to persuade others to adopt their ideas
   C their capacity to attract followers

6 Bill mentions ball point pens in order to illustrate

   A the speed with which technology has developed.
   B the negative attitude of some people to change.
   C the possible existence of a hidden market.

Part 2

You will hear an airline pilot called Rebecca Martin talking on the radio about a typical day in her job.

For questions **7–15**, complete the sentences with a word or short phrase.

___

Rebecca says that **(7)** .... are a type of bird that can cause

serious problems to aircraft.

Unlike other members of the crew, Rebecca is relieved there won't be a

(8) .... in Athens.

She says that sometimes there is someone with the title of

(9) .... on board for long haul flights.

The co-pilot bases his decision regarding **(10)** .... requirements

on various criteria.

Rebecca says that to become a pilot nowadays, it is essential to have a

(11) ...., which was not the case when she started.

She uses the phrase a **(12)** .... to describe her early attitude

towards travelling.

She thinks pilots must have what she refers to as a **(13)** ....

in order to command authority.

Having the opportunity for a **(14)** .... is a perk of the job that

Rebecca enjoyed recently for the first time.

Rebecca mentions the problem of having to work what she calls

(15) ...., which also impacts on colleagues. .

Part 3

You will hear a radio interview with Olivia Glydon and Ron Partridge, who are hyperpolyglots, people who can speak many languages.

For questions **16–20**, choose the answer (**A**, **B**, **C** or **D**) which fits best according to what you hear.

16 Olivia and Ron both say that their motivation for learning so many languages is

   A the possibility of communicating with people around the world.

   B their fascination with language systems.

   C their ability to master languages extremely quickly.

   D the challenge of achieving native speaker fluency.

17 What did Ron learn about hyperpolyglots when he was researching his book?

   A They do not have any special genetic features.

   B They usually have a history of multi-lingualism in the family.

   C They are part of a relatively recent phenomenon.

   D They usually focus on the same group of languages.

18 When discussing reactions to their hyperpolyglotism, Ron agrees with Olivia that

   A people often make the wrong assumptions about their personalities.

   B it is surprising how much attention they attract.

   C people cannot see the point of learning so many languages.

   D it is touching how eager people are to help them.

19 How does Olivia feel about spending so much time on the internet?

   A proud of the intensity with which she studies

   B defensive about the choices she makes

   C worried that she is becoming isolated from her friends

   D embarrassed about her enjoyment of soap operas and chat shows

20 What point does Ron make about one East Asian language?

   A He finds it particularly appropriate in one situation.

   B He hopes to keep it alive for posterity.

   C It has not kept up with modern developments.

   D It has a special religious significance among its speakers.

Part 4

You will hear five short extracts in which people are talking about commuting

TASK ONE

For questions **21–25**, choose from the list **(A–H)** what general concern each speaker has about commuting.

TASK TWO

For questions **26–30**, choose from the list **(A–H)** how each speaker feels now about their journey.

While you listen, you must complete both tasks.

A the unproductive use of time	
B the possible cost to mental health	
C the lack of investment in public transport	Speaker 1 ☐ 21
D the harm to the environment	Speaker 2 ☐ 22
E the potential risk of injury	Speaker 3 ☐ 23
F the tiredness it causes	Speaker 4 ☐ 24
G the difficulty in avoiding car use	Speaker 5 ☐ 25
H the increasing expense	

A pleased that it is relatively short	
B grateful to have some time for reflection	
C frustrated by fellow commuters	Speaker 1 ☐ 26
D resigned to making the best of it	Speaker 2 ☐ 27
E aware of the health benefits	Speaker 3 ☐ 28
F hopeful of a change in routine	Speaker 4 ☐ 29
G determined not to continue commuting	Speaker 5 ☐ 30
H appreciative of the surroundings	

SPEAKING (16 minutes)

There are two examiners. One (the interlocutor) conducts the test, providing you with the necessary materials and explaining what you have to do. The other examiner (the assessor) will be introduced to you, but then takes no further part in the interaction.

Part 1 (2 minutes)

The interlocutor first asks you and your partner a few questions which focus on information about yourselves.

Part 2 (4 minutes)

In this part of the test you and your partner are asked to talk together. The interlocutor places a set of pictures on the table in front of you. There may be only one picture in the set or as many as seven pictures. This stimulus provides the basis for a discussion. The interlocutor first asks an introductory question which focuses on two of the pictures (or in the case of a single picture, on aspects of the picture). After about a minute, the interlocutor gives you both a decision-making task based on the same set of pictures.

The pictures for Part 2 are on page C5 of the colour section.

Part 3 (10 minutes)

You are each given the opportunity to talk for two minutes, to comment after your partner has spoken and to take part in a more general discussion.

The interlocutor gives you a card with a question written on it and asks you to talk about it for two minutes. After you have spoken, the interlocutor asks you both another question related to the topic on the card, addressing your partner first. This procedure is repeated, so that your partner receives a card and speaks for two minutes and a follow-up question is asked.

Finally, the interlocutor asks some further questions, which lead to a discussion on a general theme related to the subjects already covered in Part 3.

The cards for Part 3 are on pages C6–C7 of the colour section.

Speaking test frames

Test 1

Note: In the examination, there will be both an assessor and an interlocutor in the room.

The visual material for Part 2 is on page C2 in the colour section of the Student's Book. The prompt cards for Part 3 are on pages C6 and C7 in the colour section of the Student's Book.

Part 1   (2 minutes / 3 minutes for groups of three)

Interlocutor: Good morning / afternoon / evening. My name is ………. and this is my colleague ………. And your names are ………. ? Could I have your mark sheets, please?

Thank you.

First of all, we'd like to know something about you.

Where are you from, (*Candidate A*)? And you, (*Candidate B*)?

[*address Candidate B*] Are you working or studying at the moment?

[*address Candidate A*] And you?

Select a further question for each candidate:

- You've said you're from (*candidate's home town/area*). How interested are you in its history?
- How good are you at relaxing?
- Do you use the internet much for your studies?
- How much interest do you take in international news?
- What would your dream holiday be?
- Will English play an important role in your future career?

Candidates: ....

Interlocutor: Thank you.

Part 2   (approximately 4 minutes / 6 minutes for groups of three)   *Class discussion – The value of information*

Interlocutor: Now, in this part of the test you're going to do something together. Here are some pictures of people in different situations.

*Place picture sheet for Test 1 (page C2) in front of the candidates. Select **two** of the pictures for the candidates to look at*.*

First, I'd like you to look at pictures * and * and talk together about which picture interests you more.

You have about a minute for this, so don't worry if I interrupt you.

(*2 minutes for groups of three*)

Candidates:
🕐 *1 minute*
(*2 minutes for groups of three*) ....

Interlocutor: Thank you. Now look at all the pictures.

I'd like you to imagine that some students are going to have a discussion on the value of information. These pictures will be used as the basis for this discussion.

Talk together about the value of information in these situations. Then suggest other situations they might discuss in which information is important.

You have about three minutes to talk about this. (*4 minutes for groups of three*)

Candidates:
🕐 *3 minutes*
(*4 minutes for groups of three*) ....

Interlocutor: Thank you. *Retrieve picture sheet.*

Part 3 (approximately 10 minutes)   *Cooperation*

Interlocutor: Now, in this part of the test you're each going to talk on your own for about two minutes. You need to listen while your partner is speaking because you'll be asked to comment afterwards.

So, (*Candidate A*), I'm going to give you a card with a question written on it and I'd like you to tell us what you think. There are also some ideas on the card for you to use if you like.

All right? Here is your card, and a copy for you (*Candidate B*).

Hand over a copy of prompt card 1a (page C6) to both candidates.

Remember (*Candidate A*), you have about two minutes to talk before we join in.

[*Allow up to 10 seconds before saying, if necessary:* Would you like to begin now?]

Candidate A: ....
🕐 *2 minutes*

Interlocutor: Thank you.

Interlocutor:	*Ask **one** of the following questions to Candidate B:*

- Why do some people prefer not to be part of a team?
- Do some types of activity require more cooperation than others?
- Is it more important to encourage children to be cooperative or to be competitive?

> *Invite Candidate A to join in by selecting one of the following prompts:*
>
> - What do you think?
> - Do you agree?
> - How about you?

Candidates: 🕐 *1 minute*	………………………………………………………....…......………
Interlocutor:	Thank you. *Retrieve cards.*
Interlocutor:	Now (*Candidate B*), it's your turn to be given a question. Here is your card, and a copy for you (*Candidate A*).

Hand over a copy of prompt card 1b (page C7) to both candidates.

Remember (*Candidate B*), you have about two minutes to tell us what you think, and there are some ideas on the card for you to use if you like. All right?

[*Allow up to 10 seconds before saying, if necessary:* Would you like to begin now?]

Candidate B: 🕐 *2 minutes*	……………………………………………….........…......………
Interlocutor:	Thank you.
Interlocutor:	*Ask **one** of the following questions to Candidate A:*

- Do you prefer to study or work independently or in a group?
- What can different countries learn from one another?
- What do you think is the best size of group for effective learning?

> *Invite Candidate B to join in by selecting one of the following prompts:*
>
> - What do you think?
> - Do you agree?
> - How about you?

Candidates: 🕐 *1 minute*	…………………………………………………….........………
Interlocutor:	Thank you. *Retrieve cards.*

Interlocutor: Now, to finish the test, we're going to talk about 'cooperation' in general.

Address a selection of the following questions to both candidates:

- In today's world, knowledge can be shared very quickly. What effect does this have?
- In a global world, should there be one global language?..... (Why? / Why not?)
- Some people say it's better to travel with other people than independently. What do you think?
- Do you think governments always achieve more when they work together?..... (Why? / Why not?)
- In what ways do people need to cooperate with one another when they live in a community?
- How do companies benefit from sponsoring other institutions such as sports clubs or schools?
- Nowadays many small companies find it difficult to survive on their own. Why do you think this is?

Candidates: ....

🕐 *up to 4 minutes*

Interlocutor: Thank you. That is the end of the test.

Test 2

Note: In the examination, there will be both an assessor and an interlocutor in the room.

The visual material for Part 2 is on pages C3 in the colour section of the Student's Book. The prompt cards for Part 3 are on pages C6 and C7 in the colour section of the Student's Book.

Part 1 (2 minutes / 3 minutes for groups of three)

Interlocutor:	Good morning / afternoon / evening. My name is .... and this is my colleague .... And your names are .... ?
	Thank you.
	First of all, we'd like to know something about you.
	Where are you from, (*Candidate A*)? And you, (*Candidate B*)?
	[*address Candidate B*] Are you working or studying at the moment?
	[*address Candidate A*] And you?
	Select a further question for each candidate:

- You've said you're from (*candidate's home town/area*). How interested are you in its history?
- How good are you at relaxing?
- Do you use the internet much for your studies?
- How much interest do you take in international news?
- What would your dream holiday be?
- Will English play an important role in your future career?

Candidates:	....
Interlocutor:	Thank you.

Part 2 (approximately 4 minutes / 6 minutes for groups of three)   *Magazine article – Control*

Interlocutor:	Now, in this part of the test you're going to do something together. Here are some pictures of people in different situations.
	*Place picture sheet for Test 2 (page C3) in front of the candidates. Select **two** of the pictures for the candidates to look at*.*
	First, I'd like you to look at pictures * and * and talk together about what sounds you might hear in these situations.
	You have about a minute for this, so don't worry if I interrupt you. (*2 minutes for groups of three*)

Candidates:
⏱ *1 minute*
(*2 minutes for groups of three*) ....

Interlocutor: Thank you. Now look at all the pictures.

I'd like you to imagine that a magazine is planning an article on aspects of control in our lives. These pictures will be used to illustrate the article.

Talk together about the different aspects of control shown in these pictures. Then suggest one other type of control that could be included in the article.

You have about three minutes to talk about this. (*4 minutes for groups of three*)

Candidates:
🕐 *3 minutes*
(*4 minutes for groups of three*) ....

Interlocutor: Thank you. *Retrieve picture sheet.*

Part 3 (approximately 10 minutes)   *Events*

Interlocutor: Now, in this part of the test you're each going to talk on your own for about two minutes. You need to listen while your partner is speaking because you'll be asked to comment afterwards.

So (*Candidate A*), I'm going to give you a card with a question written on it and I'd like you to tell us what you think. There are also some ideas on the card for you to use if you like.

All right? Here is your card, and a copy for you (*Candidate B*).

Hand over a copy of prompt card 2a (page C6) to both candidates.

Remember (*Candidate A*), you have about two minutes to talk before we join in.

[*Allow up to 10 seconds before saying, if necessary:* Would you like to begin now?]

Candidate A:
🕐 *2 minutes*   ....

Interlocutor: Thank you.

Interlocutor: *Ask **one** of the following questions to Candidate B:*

- Sometimes the preparation for a celebration is more enjoyable than the event itself. Why do you think this is?
- What makes an event more memorable, the people or the place?
- How do you record the special occasions in your life?

> *Invite Candidate A to join in by selecting one of the following prompts:*
>
> - What do you think?
> - Do you agree?
> - How about you?

Candidates:

🕐 *1 minute*   ....

Interlocutor: Thank you. *Retrieve cards.*

Interlocutor: Now (*Candidate B*), it's your turn to be given a question. Here is your card, and a copy for you (*Candidate A*).

Hand over a copy of prompt card 2b (page C7) to both candidates.

Remember (*Candidate B*), you have about two minutes to tell us what you think, and there are some ideas on the card for you to use if you like. All right?

[*Allow up to 10 seconds before saying, if necessary:* Would you like to begin now?]

Candidate B:

🕐 *2 minutes*   ....

Interlocutor: Thank you.

Interlocutor: *Ask **one** of the following questions to Candidate A:*

- Should all children be expected to learn about history at school?
- Is it more important for children to learn about their own country's history or world history?
- Should history teaching focus less on people in power and more on the lives of ordinary people?

> *Invite Candidate B to join in by selecting one of the following prompts:*
>
> - What do you think?
> - Do you agree?
> - How about you?

Candidates:

🕐 *1 minute*   ....

Interlocutor: Thank you. *Retrieve cards.*

Interlocutor: Now, to finish the test, we're going to talk about 'events' in general.

Address a selection of the following questions to both candidates:

- What is the appeal of a major international sporting event?
- Some people say the media focuses too much on negative events. Do you agree?
- What role does music play in how we experience important occasions?
- Today, news of important events can spread around the world very quickly. Is this a good thing in your view?
- Why are so many people interested in the daily events of famous people's lives?
- Which recent technological advance has had the greatest impact on the way we live today? ..... (Why do you say that?)

Candidates: ....

🕐 *up to 4 minutes*

Interlocutor: Thank you. That is the end of the test.

Test 3

Note: In the examination, there will be both an assessor and an interlocutor in the room.

The visual material for Part 2 is on page C4 in the colour section of the Student's Book. The prompt cards for Part 3 are on pages C6 and C7 in the colour section of the Student's Book.

Part 1 (2 minutes / 3 minutes for groups of three)

Interlocutor:	Good morning / afternoon / evening. My name is .... and this is my colleague .... And your names are .... ?
	Thank you.
	First of all, we'd like to know something about you.
	Where are you from, (*Candidate A*)? And you, (*Candidate B*)?
	[*address Candidate B*] Are you working or studying at the moment?
	[*address Candidate A*] And you?
	Select a further question for each candidate:

- You've said you're from (*candidate's home town/area*). How interested are you in its history?
- How good are you at relaxing?
- Do you use the internet much for your studies?
- How much interest do you take in international news?
- What would your dream holiday be?
- Will English play an important role in your future career?

Candidates:	....
Interlocutor:	Thank you.

Part 2 (approximately 4 minutes /   *Company planning –*
        6 minutes for groups of three)   *New employees*

Interlocutor:	Now, in this part of the test you're going to do something together. Here are some pictures of people in different situations.
	*Place picture sheet for Test 3 (page C4) in front of the candidates. Select **two** of the pictures for the candidates to look at*.*
	First, I'd like you to look at pictures * and * and talk together about what might happen in the next 30 seconds.
	You have about a minute for this, so don't worry if I interrupt you. *(2 minutes for groups of three)*

Candidates:
🕐 *1 minute*
(2 minutes for
groups of three) ....

96

Interlocutor:	Thank you. Now look at all the pictures.
	I'd like you to imagine that a company is considering different ways of training new employees.
	Talk together about how effective the methods shown in these pictures can be in training new employees. Then suggest one method that would <u>not</u> be effective.
	You have about three minutes to talk about this. (*4 minutes for groups of three*)
Candidates: 🕐 *3 minutes* (*4 minutes for groups of three*)	....
Interlocutor:	Thank you. *Retrieve picture sheet.*

Part 3 (approximately 10 minutes)   *Chance*

Interlocutor:	Now, in this part of the test you're each going to talk on your own for about two minutes. You need to listen while your partner is speaking because you'll be asked to comment afterwards.
	So (*Candidate A*), I'm going to give you a card with a question written on it and I'd like you to tell us what you think. There are also some ideas on the card for you to use if you like.
	All right? Here is your card, and a copy for you (*Candidate B*).
	Hand over a copy of prompt card 3a (page C6) to both candidates.
	Remember (*Candidate A*), you have about two minutes to talk before we join in.
	[*Allow up to 10 seconds before saying, if necessary:* Would you like to begin now?]
Candidate A: 🕐 *2 minutes*	....
Interlocutor:	Thank you.
Interlocutor:	*Ask **one** of the following questions to Candidate B:*

- Do you prefer to plan or to act spontaneously?
- Why do some people prefer not to take chances?
- Are chance encounters or events more fun than planned ones?

> *Invite Candidate A to join in by selecting one of the following prompts:*
>
> - What do you think?
> - Do you agree?
> - How about you?

Candidates:	
🕐 *1 minute*	....

Interlocutor: Thank you. *Retrieve cards.*

Interlocutor: Now (*Candidate B*), it's your turn to be given a question. Here is your card, and a copy for you (*Candidate A*).

        Hand over a copy of prompt card 3b (page C7) to both candidates.

        Remember (*Candidate B*), you have about two minutes to tell us what you think, and there are some ideas on the card for you to use if you like. All right?

        [*Allow up to 10 seconds before saying, if necessary:* Would you like to begin now?]

Candidate B:	
🕐 *2 minutes*	....

Interlocutor: Thank you.

Interlocutor: *Ask **one** of the following questions to Candidate A:*

- How important do you think luck is in life?
- Is it better to be successful through hard work or through good luck?
- Is it sometimes good to have a routine?

> *Invite Candidate B to join in by selecting one of the following prompts:*
>
> - What do you think?
> - Do you agree?
> - How about you?

Candidates:	
🕐 *1 minute*	....

Interlocutor: Thank you. *Retrieve cards.*

Interlocutor: Now, to finish the test, we're going to talk about 'chance' in general.

        Address a selection of the following questions to both candidates:

- Are there some things in life that have to be left to chance? ..... (Why? / Why not?)
- Some people say there are more opportunities for people today than ever before. What do you think?
- Does the media raise unrealistic expectations about the chances that life offers us?
- How can children be helped to deal with the unpredictability of life?
- In the past, many people stayed in the same job for most of their lives. Is this a good thing do you think?
- Is it better for towns and cities to be planned or to develop naturally? ..... (Why do you say that?)

Candidates: ....

🕐 *up to 4 minutes*

Interlocutor: Thank you. That is the end of the test.

Test 4

Note: In the examination, there will be both an assessor and an interlocutor in the room.

The visual material for Part 2 is on page C5 in the colour section of the Student's Book. The prompt cards for Part 3 are on pages C6 and C7 in the colour section of the Student's Book.

Part 1 (2 minutes / 3 minutes for groups of three)

Interlocutor:	Good morning / afternoon / evening. My name is .... and this is my colleague .... And your names are .... ?
	Thank you.
	First of all, we'd like to know something about you.
	Where are you from, (*Candidate A*)? And you, (*Candidate B*)?
	[*address Candidate B*] Are you working or studying at the moment?
	[*address Candidate A*] And you?
	Select a further question for each candidate:

- You've said you're from (*candidate's home town/area*). How interested are you in its history?
- How good are you at relaxing?
- Do you use the internet much for your studies?
- How much interest do you take in international news?
- What would your dream holiday be?
- Will English play an important role in your future career?

Candidates:	....
Interlocutor:	Thank you.

Part 2 (approximately 4 minutes / 6 minutes for groups of three)   *TV documentary series – Lifestyles*

Interlocutor:	Now, in this part of the test you're going to do something together. Here is a picture of people in a specific situation.
	Place picture sheet for Test 4 (C5) in front of the candidates.
	First, I'd like you to look at the picture and talk together about how the people might be feeling.
	You have about a minute for this, so don't worry if I interrupt you. (*2 minutes for groups of three*)
Candidates: ⏲ *1 minute* (*2 minutes for groups of three*)	....
Interlocutor:	Thank you. Now look at both the pictures.

I'd like you to imagine that a television company is planning a series of three documentaries on lifestyles today. These pictures illustrate the topic of the first programme.

Talk together about changes that are taking place in peoples' lifestyles today, as shown in the picture. Then suggest two other aspects of modern lifestyles that should be included in the rest of the series.

You have about three minutes to talk about this. (*4 minutes for groups of three*)

Candidates:
🕐 *3 minutes*
(*4 minutes for groups of three*) ....

Interlocutor: Thank you. *Retrieve the picture sheet.*

Part 3 (approximately 10 minutes)   *Authority*

Interlocutor: Now, in this part of the test you're each going to talk on your own for about two minutes. You need to listen while your partner is speaking because you'll be asked to comment afterwards.

So (*Candidate A*), I'm going to give you a card with a question written on it and I'd like you to tell us what you think. There are also some ideas on the card for you to use if you like.

All right? Here is your card, and a copy for you (*Candidate B*).

Hand over a copy of prompt card 4a (page C6) to both candidates.

Remember (*Candidate A*), you have about two minutes to talk before we join in.

[*Allow up to 10 seconds before saying, if necessary:* Would you like to begin now?]

Candidate A:
🕐 *2 minutes*   ....

Interlocutor: Thank you.

Interlocutor: *Ask **one** of the following questions to Candidate B:*

- Is it natural for young children to question their parents' authority?
- Do you think it is true that fathers tend to be stricter than mothers?
- At what age are children in your country expected to become independent?

> *Invite Candidate A to join in by selecting one of the following prompts:*
>
> - What do you think?
> - Do you agree?
> - How about you?

Candidates:
🕐 *1 minute*   ....

Interlocutor: Thank you. *Retrieve cards.*

Interlocutor: Now (*Candidate B*), it's your turn to be given a question. Here is your card, and a copy for you (*Candidate A*).

> *Hand over a copy of prompt card 4b (page C7) to both candidates.*

> Remember (*Candidate B*), you have about two minutes to tell us what you think, and there are some ideas on the card for you to use if you like. All right?

> [*Allow up to 10 seconds before saying, if necessary:* Would you like to begin now?]

Candidate B:
🕐 *2 minutes*   ....

Interlocutor: Thank you.

Interlocutor: *Ask **one** of the following questions to Candidate A:*

- Is it easier to manage one person or a team of people?
- What is the best way to learn how to be a manager?
- Do you think men and women have different styles of management?

> *Invite Candidate B to join in by selecting one of the following prompts:*
>
> - What do you think?
> - Do you agree?
> - How about you?

Candidates:
🕐 *1 minute*   ....

Interlocutor: Thank you. Retrieve cards.

Interlocutor: Now, to finish the test, we're going to talk about 'authority' in general.

> *Address a selection of the following questions to both candidates:*

- Is it easier to lead or to follow? ..... (Why do you think that?)
- Do teachers need to be strict to be effective?..... (Why? / Why not?)

- Why can wearing a uniform give a person added authority?
- What makes some people choose to seek positions of power?
- Would the world be a better place if there were more laws or fewer laws?.....
  (Why? / Why not?)
- In many cultures, people are given more respect as they grow
  older. How do you feel about this?

Candidates: ....
up to 🕐 *4 minutes*

Interlocutor: Thank you. That is the end of the test.

Marks and results

Reading and Use of English

One mark is given for each correct answer in Parts 1–3 and 7. Two marks are given for each correct answer for Parts 5–6. Up to two marks are awarded for Part 4. The total score is then weighted to 80 marks for the whole Reading and Use of English paper.

Writing assessment

Examiners mark tasks using Assessment Scales that were developed with explicit reference to the Common European Framework of Reference for Languages (CEFR). The scales, which are used across the spectrum of Cambridge English Language Assessment's General and Business English Writing tests, consist of four subscales: Content, Communicative Achievement, Organisation, and Language:

Content focuses on how well the candidate has fulfilled the task, in other words if they have done what they were asked to do.

Communicative Achievement focuses on how appropriate the writing is for the task and whether the candidate has used the appropriate register.

Organisation focuses on the way the candidate puts together the piece of writing, in other words if it is logical and ordered.

Language focuses on vocabulary and grammar. This includes the range of language as well as how accurate it is.

Responses are marked on each subscale from 0 to 5. The subscale Content is common to all levels:

	Content
5	All content is relevant to the task. Target reader is fully informed.
3	Minor irrelevances and/or omissions may be present. Target reader is on the whole informed.
1	Irrelevances and misinterpretation of task may be present. Target reader is minimally informed.
0	Content is totally irrelevant Target reader is not informed.

The remaining three subscales (Communicative Achievement, Organisation, and Language) have descriptors specific to each CEFR level:

CEFR level	Communicative Achievement	Organisation	Language
C2	Uses the conventions of the communicative task with sufficient flexibility to communicate complex ideas in an effective way, holding the target reader's attention with ease, fulfilling all communicative purposes.	Text is organised impressively and coherently using a wide range of cohesive devices and organisational patterns with complete flexibility.	Uses a wide range of vocabulary, including less common lexis, with fluency, precision, sophistication and style. Use of grammar is sophisticated, fully controlled and completely neutral. Any inaccuracies occur only as slips.
C1	Uses the conventions of the communicative task effectively to hold the target reader's attention and communicate straightforward and complex ideas, as appropriate.	Text is a well-organised, coherent whole, using a variety of cohesive devices and organisational patterns with flexibility.	Uses a range of vocabulary, including less common lexis, appropriately. Uses a range of simple and complex grammatical forms with control and flexibility. Occasional errors may be present but do not impede communication.
B2	Uses the conventions of the communicative task to hold the target reader's attention and communicate straightforward ideas.	Text is generally well organised and coherent, using a variety of linking words and cohesive devices.	Uses a range of everyday vocabulary appropriately, with occasional inappropriate use of less common lexis. Uses a range of simple and some complex grammatical forms with a good degree of control. Errors do not impede communication.
B1	Uses the conventions of the communicative task in generally appropriate ways to communicate straightforward ideas.	Text is connected and coherent, using basic linking words and a limited number of cohesive devices.	Uses everyday vocabulary generally appropriately, while occasionally overusing certain lexis. Uses simple grammatical forms with a good degree of control. While errors are noticeable, meaning can still be determined.
A2	Produces text that communicates simple ideas in simple ways.	Text is connected using basic, high-frequency linking words.	Uses basic vocabulary reasonably appropriately. Uses simple grammatical forms with some degree of control. Errors may impede meaning at times.

CPE Writing Examiners use the following Assessment Scale, extracted from the one above:

C2	Content	Communicative Achievement	Organisation	Language
5	All content is relevant to the task. Target reader is fully informed.	Demonstrates complete command of the conventions of the communicative task. Communicates complex ideas in an effective and convincing way, holding the target reader's attention with ease, fulfilling all communicative purposes.	Text is organised impressively and coherently using a wide range of cohesive devices and organisational patterns with complete flexibility.	Uses a wide range of vocabulary, including less common lexis, with fluency, precision, sophistication, and style. Use of grammar is sophisticated, fully controlled and completely natural. Any inaccuracies occur only as slips.
4	*Performance shares features of Bands 3 and 5.*			
3	Minor irrelevances and/or omissions may be present. Target reader is on the whole informed.	Uses the conventions of the communicative task with sufficient flexibility to communicate complex ideas in an effective way, holding the target reader's attention with ease, fulfilling all communicative purposes.	Text is a well-organised, coherent whole, using a variety of cohesive devices and organisational patterns with flexibility.	Uses a range of vocabulary, including less common lexis, effectively and precisely. Uses a wide range of simple and complex grammatical forms with full control, flexibility and sophistication. Errors, if present, are related to less common words and structures, or as slips.
2	*Performance shares features of Bands 1 and 3.*			
1	Irrelevances and misinterpretation of task may be present. Target reader is minimally informed.	Uses the conventions of the communicative task effectively to hold the target reader's attention and communicate straightforward and complex ideas, as appropriate.	Text is well organised and coherent, using a variety of cohesive devices and organisational patterns to generally good effect.	Uses a range of vocabulary, including less common lexis, appropriately. Uses a range of simple and complex grammatical forms with control and flexibility. Occasional errors may be present but do not impede communication.
0	Content is totally irrelevant. Target reader is not informed.	*Performance below Band 1.*		

When marking the tasks, examiners take into account length of responses. Scripts which are under- or over-length are not penalised *per se*. Responses which are too short may not have an adequate range of language and may not provide all the information that is required, while responses which are too long may contain irrelevant content and have a negative effect on the reader. These factors may affect candidates' marks on the relevant subscales.

Writing sample answers and examiner's comments

The following pieces of writing have been selected from students' answers. The samples relate to tasks in Tests 1–4. Explanatory notes have been added to show how the bands have been arrived at. The comments on Part 1 questions and Part 2 questions 5a and 5b should be read in conjunction with the Briefing Documents included in the Keys.

Sample A (Test 1, Part 1, Question 1, Essay)

Garbage is becoming a huge problem in our society. Whether it's plastic, paper or electronic devices, all of that rubbish is immediately thrown in the garbage disposal. Although we try to recycle, the amount of waste we simply throw away severely outweighs the amount of recycled rubbish. Not to mention the amazing potential of resources than can be pulled from old electronic hardware.

But why is it the case, anyways, that there's so much 'cellular waste'? Some say it's because of the ever-increasing speed of new developments in technology. Others say that it's because advertising has become more and more effective over the last couple of years. Or perhaps it is because phones are simply becoming more and more fragile and are prone to having a broken screen, a battery that runs out too quickly or any other malfunction. Electronical hardware isn't the only evil-doer, though. For example, any packaging made out of plastic cannot simply be melted into a moldable plastic; plastic doesn't work that way. Plastic bags usually end up on the garbage piles because of that.

But the biggest concern right now is, surprisingly, paper. We, as a society, use paper for everyday tasks: Whether it's writing down groceries, faxing the tax income from last month or even writing a CPE test. It is of no surprise that paper is the biggest environmental concern when one realises the sheer amount of paper that is used by humanity every day. The only reason it's not as bad as plastic is that paper is biodegradable. Paper can be made into a pulp, only to be recast into the good old A4 format we all know and love.

Now we just have to actually do that, if we wish to save our environment.

Subscale	Mark	Commentary
Content*	5	All content is relevant to the task and the target reader would be fully informed. The candidate is successful not only in summarising and commenting on the content points, but also giving their own ideas (note the discussion in the second paragraph of another possible reason for people keeping electronic devices for only a short time).
Communicative Achievement	3	Although the register and style are at times more appropriate to an article (... *the good old A4 format we all know and love* and the short, informal conclusion), the conventions of the communicative task are used with sufficient flexibility to communicate complex ideas in an effective way (note the discussion of paper in the third paragraph), holding the target reader's attention with ease, and fulfilling all communicative purposes.
Organisation	3	The text is a well-organised, coherent whole, using a variety of cohesive devices and organisational patterns with flexibility (*Although, Not to mention, But why is it the case ..., Some say it's because ..., For example, But ...., surprisingly, ..., The only reason it's ...*).
Language	3	The candidate uses a range of vocabulary, including less common lexis, effectively and precisely (*disposal, outweighs, prone to, sheer amount, pulp, recast*). The candidate also uses a wide range of simple and complex grammatical forms with full control, flexibility and sophistication. Errors are present but are related to less common words and structures (*severely outweighs, electronical hardware, evil-doer, it is of no surprise*).

* See Briefing Document, p 126. Key points from each Part 1 question are listed in a Briefing Document for markers.

Sample B (Test 1, Part 2, Question 2, Letter)

Dear Sir / Madam,

I am writing in regards to the feature in your magazine that concerns taking risks.

Risks are being taken your whole life, everywhere around you. One had to only realise that some risks may be more impactful than others.

Once upon a day, I fell in love with the most beautiful girl in the world. I was so madly in love I couldn't deal with not knowing if she loved me back. I thoughtlessly took a risk and confessed my deep feelings for her.

She didn't feel the same way, and I was devastated. A broken man, I couldn't help but feel it wasn't a risk I should have taken. Over the course of a month, however, she did fall in love with me, as a direct consequence of my leap of faith.

She admired my courage and now noticed me, discovering untold virtues in me unnoticed by anyone else. We are now happily together and wedding plans are being made.

I think it is that courage, the courage she saw in me that entices people to take risks, despite the odds not being in your favour. It is this desire to be looked up to and admired that makes our inner risk-taker tick.

In retrospective, I am so glad I build up the courage to take my risk, for if I wouldn't have, I could not stop deliberating the 'What-if's'. In life we do not regret the risks we took, but the ones we did not.

Taking risks can be a catharsis, allow you to see things clearly, and teach you something in the process. Taking a well-deliberated risk is almost always worth taking, because to think about what could have been, is so much worse than seeing what never became, knowing you took the chance.

Thus, I would like to end by encouraging all of you to take risks, or to, as Nike would say, just do it.

Yours sincerely,

Subscale	Mark	Commentary
Content	5	All content is relevant to the task. The target reader would be fully informed as to the writer's views on all four parts of the question.
Communicative Achievement	4	The candidate demonstrates a good command of the conventions of the communicative task. The letter communicates complex ideas in an effective and often quite convincing way (for example, the penultimate paragraph in which the candidate justifies the taking of risks), holding the target reader's attention with ease (note the highly engaging way in which the candidate tells their story), fulfilling all communicative purposes.
Organisation	3	The text is a well-organised, coherent whole, using a variety of cohesive devices and organisational patterns with flexibility (*however, I think it was that courage, the courage she saw in me …, despite, Thus I would like to end by …*), although there are a couple of inaccurately used devices (*Once upon a day, In retrospective*).
Language	3	The candidate uses a range of vocabulary, including less common lexis, effectively and precisely (*devastated, broken man, leap of faith, entices, the odds not being in your favour, tick, deliberating, catharsis*). The candidate also uses a wide range of simple and complex grammatical forms with full control, flexibility and sophistication (*I couldn't help but feel it wasn't a risk I should have taken; taking a well-deliberated risk is almost always worth taking, because to think about what could have been is so much worse than seeing what never became*). A few errors are present but are related to more complex and less common structures (*I am writing in regards to; if I wouldn't have*).

Sample C (Test 2, Part 1, Question 1, Essay)

Home sweet home

It is in human nature to settle down in some place and then call it home. It can be a bedsit in a run-down part of the town or a mansion in a clean suburban residential area – home is where you make it.

Throughout our lives we may have several homes. First, we live with our parents, then we might move to college, then start a family and finally we may end up in a care home. However, even in adulthood we may have to relocate several times due to e.g. a divorce, financial constraints or simply as a matter of choice.

Some people move homes easily, some suffer immensely when they are uprooted, but even people with itchy feet understand the concept of home.

What is home then? It is the most private place for every human being. It is a place where we can unwind after a stressful day by reading, spending time with the family or having a glass of wine and a family meal. Home is a private recluse, a shrine for contemplation on our own or with our loved ones. My house is my castle.

Moreover, our home speaks volumes about our personality. When we are socialising on a night out we should our public selves, but at home we present our private selves. The overall design and furnishing of our home expresses our taste, likes and dislikes, and also our attitudes in life.

Our personality also reflects itself in our willingness to share this place with others. There are people who enjoy entertaining friends at dinner parties while some people protect the sacred privacy of their precious home.

All in all, it is important to have a place we can call home and we should have sympathy for homeless people who cannot afford this luxury. As Dorothy said in the Wizard of Oz: "There is no place like home."

Subscale	Mark	Commentary
Content*	4	All content is relevant to the task. However, the target reader would not be fully informed as the third content point has been entirely omitted. Although content points one and two are dealt with fairly briefly, the candidate does well in giving their own views on the topic.
Communicative Achievement	4	The candidate demonstrates a good command of the conventions of the communicative task. The register is consistently and appropriately formal. Complex ideas are communicated highly effectively and often convincingly (note the discussion of human nature and the universality of the concept of home in the first and third paragraphs), holding the target reader's attention with ease and fulfilling all communicative purposes.
Organisation	3	The text is a well-organised, coherent whole with a variety of cohesive devices (*However, Moreover, All in all,*) and organisational patterns (*What is home, then?*) used with flexibility. Note also the fact that the essay has a good (though possibly slightly long) introduction and an effective conclusion.
Language	4	A wide range of vocabulary, including less common lexis, is used effectively and precisely, and sometimes with sophistication and style (*bedsit, run-down, financial constraints, uprooted, itchy feet, a shrine, speaks volumes, sacred*). A wide range of simple and complex grammatical forms are used with full control and flexibility, and sometimes in a way that is very natural. There is a notable lack of inaccuracies.

* See Briefing Document, p 135. Key points from each Part 1 question are listed in a Briefing Document for markers.

Sample D (Test 2, Part 2, Question 2, Report)

The aim of this report, is to outline and evaluate the sports camp using my own experience as a volunteer at this camp.

Being a coach at this sports camp, has been a very rewarding experience. My main task was to introduce the teenagers to football and hockey. Together with two other coaches, we taught the teenagers the basic rules of the sports and spent one afternoon per sport, practising the sport. During the mornings, I helped prepare lunch.

Generally, the teenagers seemed to have enjoyed the sports activities, and the overall experience. The youngsters felt like they could talk to the coaches if there was a problem, and that when a problem occurred, everyone cooperated to solve this problem. The children found that the atmosphere was very helpfull and friendly. Mostly due to those aspects, a large number of teenagers took up new sports took up new sports after our camp was finished.

The outcome of our survey was generally very positive. There was just one point of recommendation which was made several times, namely that most parents find the costs for this sports camp relatively high. They suggested making use of cheaper accomodation sites, and including a special discount on the sport a teenager may start after participating in this summer camp. We should take these suggestions very seriously, because we do not want money to be an obstacle for anyone when choosing a summer camp.

The conclusion of this report is that our recent sports camp was succesfull, but that we should find a way to make our camp cheaper.

Subscale	Mark	Commentary
Content	5	All content is relevant to the task, although the points are not covered in great depth (for example the candidate only makes one recommendation).
Communicative Achievement	2	The conventions of the communicative task are used effectively and with some flexibility to hold the reader's attention and communicate straightforward and complex ideas, as appropriate. The style and register are consistently and appropriately formal.
Organisation	2	The text is well-organised and coherent. The candidate has used a variety, but not a wide range, of cohesive devices and organisational patterns to generally good effect (*The aim of this report is to …; Generally; Mostly due to these aspects; namely that; The conclusion of this report is that …*).
Language	1	The candidate uses a range of vocabulary, including less common lexis, appropriately (*rewarding, outcome*).

The candidate also uses a range of simple and complex grammatical forms with control and flexibility. There is a notable lack of grammatical errors. However, the range of vocabulary and expression is not particularly wide or ambitious. |

Sample E (Test 3, Part 1, Question 1, Essay)

The clothes you wear will always have an impact on you and your surroundings. This goes especially for professionals such as doctors and lawyers. By wearing their distinctive uniforms, they give their clients or patients a clear non-verbal message. They show what they're doing and they can be trusted.

However, wearing a uniform won't always be solely beneficial. Sometimes one has to be trusted in a different, more personal way, and in those cases uniforms will only create distance. A psychologist for example, should probably wear informal clothing when dealing with patients.

In my opinion, one should always try to dress for the ocasion. The previous examples are all true, but you mustn't overdo it. A lawyer should wear a suit, yes, but if he or she were to show up in their black robes they wear in court, it would be slightly overwhelming.

Although I do agree that doctors should wear their uniforms when dealing with patients, there is – in my opinion – one exception: pediatricians. Most kids, especially very young ones, are afraid of doctors and hospitals. And it is the doctor's task to make them feel more comfortable. Wearing less informal clothes would be a simple, yet effective, step in that direction. If a doctor looks just like mommy or daddy, rather than some professor from TV, what's there to be scared about?

In conclusion, you could say that clothes make a difference, both positively and negatively.

Clothing can be a professional's way of showing he knows what he's doing or saying he too is just another human being.

Just be careful not to overdo it, for that is one of the easiest ways to lose all credibility.

Subscale	Mark	Commentary
Content*	4	All content is relevant to the task. However, the target reader would not be fully informed as the candidate does not deal with the fourth point regarding wearing formal clothes at important public occasions. The first point is dealt with implicitly, with much more attention given to the third content point.
Communicative Achievement	3	The candidate uses the conventions of the communicative task with sufficient flexibility to communicate complex ideas in an effective way, holding the target reader's attention with ease (note the paragraph in which the candidate discusses what paediatricians should wear) and fulfilling all communicative purposes. There are a few lapses into a slightly informal style in places that might be more appropriate to an article rather than an essay (*what's there to be scared about? Just be careful not to overdo it*).
Organisation	3	The text is a well-organised, coherent whole, despite some over-paragraphing towards the end, using a variety of cohesive devices and organisational patterns with flexibility (*This goes especially for …; However; The previous examples are all …; Although I do agree that …; In conclusion*).
Language	3	The candidate uses a range of vocabulary, including less common lexis, effectively and precisely (*distinctive, non-verbal message, show up, black robes, overwhelming, lose all credibility*). They also use a wide range of simple and complex grammatical forms with full control, flexibility and sophistication.

* See Briefing Document, p 144. Key points from each Part 1 question are listed in a Briefing Document for markers.

Sample F (Test 3, Part 2, Question 2, Article)

When I think of a situation in which I felt really happy, I immeadiatly think of the time when I was eleven years old. On Friday afternoons, just before the start of the weekend, my friends and I always went to the house of one of us. Our goal was to write and make our own school paper, but usually we just fooled around, and had so much fun that afterwards our stomachs hurted from all the laughing we did.

Of course, people always consider their childhoods as the time they felt happiest. Not only because they were so care-free as children, but also because they romantisised their memories. Nevertheless, we should learn from children if we want to be as happy as they usually are. Living in the moment and not worry to much seems really to contribute feelings of happiness for most people.

However, adults have responsibilities, which means they have to worry sometimes. Otherwise, a well-organised civilisation like ours wouldn't be able to excist. But sometimes it's good to let all the stress go, just relax and don't think to much about anything but the present. It is not coincidence that there is a growing number of people taking yoga and meditation classes, to reduce their stress levels and feel free.

So overall, my conclusion is that the key to happiness is being child-like care-free. And even though a little stress can do no harm, and is sometimes even beneficial, our aim should be to stop worrying and start living in the moment. After all, what's the use of being stressed all the time because of your job, when it will only makes you unhappy? Stop thinking, start living, and you'll feel just as happy as when you were a care-free child.

Subscale	Mark	Commentary
Content	4	All content is relevant to the task. The third part of the question has not been explicitly addressed, with only a somewhat oblique reference to it in the final paragraph.
Communicative Achievement	3	The candidate uses the conventions of the communicative task with sufficient flexibility to communicate complex ideas in an effective way (note the analysis of childhood in the second paragraph and the discussion of stress and living in the present in the third and fourth paragraphs), holding the reader's attention with ease and fulfilling all communicative purposes. The candidate writes in an engaging and lively way appropriate to an article in a magazine, addressing the reader directly and giving them friendly advice (... *what's the use of being stressed all the time because of your job, when it will only makes you unhappy?*).
Organisation	3	The text is a well-organised, coherent whole, using a variety of cohesive devices and organisational patterns with flexibility (*Of course; Not only because they ...; but also because ...; Nevertheless; However; So overall, my conclusion is that ...; After all*).
Language	2	The candidate uses a range of vocabulary, including less common lexis, appropriately and sometimes effectively and precisely (*fooled around, coincidence, meditation*). However, the range is not wide and some ambitious words are over-used (*care-free*) or misspelt (*romantisised*). The candidate also uses a wide range of simple and complex grammatical forms with control and flexibility, and occasionally with sophistication (for example, ... *adults have responsibilities, which means they have to worry sometimes. Otherwise, a well-organised civilisation like ours wouldn't be able to excist*; and also ... *even though a little stress can do no harm, and is sometimes even beneficial, our aim should be to stop worrying and start living in the moment*). Occasional errors are present but do not impede communication (*Our stomachs hurted; Living in the moment and not worry too much seems really to contribute to feelings of happiness ...; It is not coincidence that there is ...*). There are a few spelling errors (*excist, immeadiatly*).

Sample G (Test 4, Part 1, Question 1, Essay)

Memories have a different meaning for every person. For some, they are a way of connection with others – such as friends. For others, they are of assistance in finding certain facts. Moreover, they shape us to who we are, for all that we have been through has been stored neatly in our heads.

However, there are downsides to every example given in the previous paragraph. Memories are able to drag you into your past, to a time where – for example – everything was more beautiful. For some, it is so hard to return to the present, or to admit that those things really *do* belong in the past, that they get depressed. Because all of this happens in the head no cure is known except speaking about it with another. Another downside from memories is the fact that no one thinks the same and because of this no one remembers the same: some may remember a certain event in a completely different light than another. This proves that knowledge or facts cannot always be gained by asking witnesses to share their memories about a certain crime. As for the downside to the last example of memories, the fact that they make you who you really are: bad memories have the tendency to be remembered as well. This means the experiences you would have rather not been through, also have a say in a person's personality.

Still, by knowing how these situations can be avoided, we can enjoy our memories as much and as long as possible. Those who are elderly will give you this tip over and over, since they know how fast memories can disappear on you.

As much as we love our memories, it is necessary to be aware of the negative aspects of sinking into them.

Cherish your memory, but live in the present.

Subscale	Mark	Commentary
Content*	5	All content is relevant to the task. The target reader is fully informed.
Communicative Achievement	3	The candidate uses the conventions of the communicative task with sufficient flexibility to communicate complex ideas in an effective way (note in particular the strong and well-argued second paragraph dealing with some of the problems people have with memories), holding the target reader's attention with ease, fulfilling all communicative purposes.
Organisation	3	The text is a well-organised, coherent whole, using a variety of cohesive devices and organisational patterns with flexibility (*Moreover; However, there are downsides to every example given in the previous paragraph; for example; Another downside …; This proves that …; As for; This means …; Still*). The candidate does not deal with the content points in the order in which they appear in the input texts, but skilfully weaves them together, for example combining points 2 and 4 in one paragraph because they are both negative in nature, and then returning to point 2 at the end of the essay to help give it a strong conclusion.
Language	3	The candidate uses a range of vocabulary, including less common lexis, effectively and precisely (*shape, stored neatly, drag, have a say in, tip, sinking, cherish*), although not a wide range. The candidate also uses a wide range of simple and complex grammatical forms with full control, flexibility and sophistication (*As much as we love our memories, it is necessary to be aware of the negative aspects of sinking into them*, and *This means the experiences you would have rather not been through also have a say in a person's personality*).

* See Briefing Document, p 152. Key points from each Part 1 question are listed in a Briefing Document for markers.

Sample H (Test 4, Part 2, Question 4, Review)

Take your chance in the job market

Last week, I had the chance to attend a jobs fair which was targeted at university students in their final year who are ready to launch into the world of work. Major international companies presented themselves; the majority being the market leaders in the field of technology, but also big retailers, supermarket and fast-food chains and restaurant franchises were present.

The companies that caught my attention most were IBM and A-Hold. Both of them attracted the attendees by their highly professional presentations and conduct.

IBM is one of the major computing companies, nevertheless, they also offer a variety of positions in their company structure, such as managerial and secretarial posts. IBM is a well-established corporation which enables their employees to climb the career ladder providing they stay loyal to the company. Their stall was by far the biggest and the most high-tech in the fair and their production was flawless. Young and well-informed staff dressed in matching and perfectly-fitting uniforms were patiently answering all questions the visitors asked. Every half an hour they played a pre-recorded presentation regarding the company history, which looked simply amazing. The visitors could also use an interactive screen why they could find all the information desired.

The other company which impressed me was A-Hold, It is a supermarket chain which comes from the Netherlands but operates throughout Europe. One would expect that they would advertise only the not very well-paid jobs on the supermarket floor. I was surprised to see that this company is also seeking well-qualified people to join their staff. They offer in-company trainings and internships which increase the changes to be hired full-time for a junior and after only 2 years to senior management position!

Their presentation included a great amount of 'freebies', such as key rings, notepads, calendars but also backpacks and manicure sets.

In contrast, some of the companies underestimated the importance of good PR. Their stalls looked boring and without any invention. It is a shame because some of them advertised really appealing job positions, but good marketing is essential these days and it takes some effort to be noticed in the market. Leaflets and black and white prints are not going to impress the youth of this generation.

To sum up, the fair was a success. I was passing groups of students chatting enthusiastically about various companies they had encountered. Such events are definitely useful for students as they could help tackle the growing problem of unemployment amongst the young.

Subscale	Mark	Commentary
Content	5	All content is relevant to the task. The target reader is fully informed.
Communicative Achievement	4	The candidate demonstrates a good command of the conventions of the communicative task. The candidate communicates complex ideas in an effective and sometimes convincing way (note the paragraph describing the IBM stall and the paragraph that criticised the poor marketing by other companies), holding the reader's attention with ease and fulfilling all communicative purposes.
Organisation	3	The text is a well-organised, coherent whole, using a variety but not a wide range, of cohesive devices and organisational patterns with flexibility (*nevertheless; The other company which impressed me; In contrast; To sum up; Such events*).
Language	4	The candidate uses a wide range of vocabulary, including less common lexis, effectively and precisely and sometimes with fluency and some evidence of style (*market leaders, restaurant franchises, career ladder, flawless, freebies, manicure sets, tackle*). The candidate also uses a wide range of simple and complex grammatical forms with full control, flexibility and sophistication, and sometimes in a way that is very natural.

Listening

One mark is given for each correct answer. The total is weighted to give a mark out of 40 for the paper. In Part 2 spelling errors are not allowed.

For security reasons, several versions of the Listening paper are used at each administration of the examination. Before grading, the performance of the candidates in each of the versions is compared and marks adjusted to compensate for any imbalance in levels of difficulty.

Speaking

Assessment

Candidates are assessed on their own individual performance and not in relation to each other, according to the following five analytical criteria: grammatical resource, lexical resource, discourse management, pronunciation and interactive communication. These criteria are interpreted at level C2 of the CEFR. Assessment is based on performance in the whole test and is not related to particular parts of the test.

Both examiners assess the candidates. The assessor applies detailed, analytical scales, and the interlocutor applies the global achievement scale, which is based on the analytical scales.

Analytical scales

Grammatical resource

This refers to the accurate application of grammar rules and the effective arrangement of words in utterances. At level C2 of the CEFR a wide range of grammatical forms should be used appropriately and competently. Performance is viewed in terms of the overall effectiveness of the language used.

Lexical resource

This refers to the candidate's ability to use a wide and appropriate range of vocabulary to meet task requirements. At level C2 of the CEFR, the tasks require candidates to express precise meanings, attitudes and opinions and to be able to convey abstract ideas. Performance is viewed in terms of the overall effectiveness of the language used.

Discourse management

This refers to the candidate's ability to link utterances together to form coherent monologue and contributions to dialogue. The utterances should be relevant to the tasks and to preceding utterances in the discourse. The discourse produced should be at a level of complexity appropriate to level C2 of the CEFR and the utterances should be arranged logically to develop the themes or arguments required by the tasks. The extent of contributions should be appropriate, i.e. long or short as required at a particular point in the dynamic development of the discourse in order to achieve the task.

Pronunciation

This refers to the candidate's ability to produce easily comprehensible utterances to fulfil the task requirements. At level C2 of the CEFR, acceptable pronunciation should be achieved by the appropriate use of strong and weak syllables, the smooth linking of words and the effective highlighting of information-bearing words. Intonation, which includes the use of a sufficiently wide pitch range, should be used effectively to convey meaning and articulation of individual sounds should be sufficiently clear for words to be understood. Examiners put themselves in the position of the non-EFL specialist and assess the overall impact of the communication and the degree of effort required to understand the candidate.

Interactive communication

This refers to the candidate's ability to take an active part in the development of the discourse, showing sensitivity to turn taking and without undue hesitation. It requires the ability to participate competently in the range of interactive situations in the test and to develop discussions on a range of topics by initiating and responding appropriately. It also refers to the deployment of strategies to maintain and repair interaction at an appropriate level throughout the test so that the tasks can be fulfilled.

Global achievement scale

This scale refers to the candidate's overall effectiveness in dealing with the tasks in the three parts of the Cambridge English: Proficiency Speaking Test.

Marks

Marks for each scale are awarded out of five and are subsequently weighted to produce a final mark out of 40.

Test 1 Key

Reading and Use of English (1 hour 30 minutes)

Part 1

1 D   2 B   3 C   4 A   5 A   6 D   7 C   8 B

Part 2

9 come   10 because   11 until   12 tall   13 Providing
14 make   15 never   16 vain

Part 3

17 evolutionary   18 significance   19 attachment   20 helplessness
21 advantageous   22 injustice(s)   23 involuntarily   24 undeniable

Part 4

25 will be taken | into account
26 difficulty (in) coming up | with (the) answers to
27 were put in | charge of
28 had given up hope | of Sam Bowker
29 bore no | resemblance to
30 what his sister's | opposition to

Part 5

31 A   32 B   33 A   34 D   35 B   36 A

Part 6

37 C   38 F   39 H   40 A   41 D   42 G   43 E

Part 7

44 B   45 A   46 A   47 D   48 D   49 B   50 C
51 C   52 A   53 C

Writing (1 hour 30 minutes)

Briefing Document

Question 1

Content
Essay must refer to and evaluate the following points:
- many of us throw away a huge amount of stuff – some can be recycled
- whether enough is being done to recycle is debatable
- advertising persuades us to discard electronic products after a short time
- people wish to keep up with the latest developments in communication technology
- writer's own ideas on topic.

Question 5a

Content
Clear reference to the book chosen
Description of Ethan and Edward and their roles in the book

Range
Language of describing, analysing, narrating

Appropriacy of register and format
Register and format appropriate to that of review

Organisation and cohesion
Clear organisation and development of ideas
Adequate use of paragraphing

Target reader
Would understand the roles played by Ethan and Edward

Question 5b

Content
Article should include:
Focus on Roxanne's role in the house
A description of the connection between music and love in Roxanne's relationships
with other people in the house

Range
Language of description
Language of analysis

Appropriacy of register and format
Article format
Register consistently appropriate for international literary magazine

Organisation and cohesion
Clear presentation and development of ideas in well-organised prose
Adequate use of linking and paragraphing

Target reader
Would understand Roxanne's role in the house and the connection between music
and love in her relationships

Listening (approximately 40 minutes)

Part 1

1 A   2 C   3 B   4 C   5 C   6 B

Part 2

7 insulation   8 (old) cans   9 storage heaters   10 off the grid
11 community centre / center   12 (car) tyres / tires   13 lizards
14 leaking roofs   15 Trash Pirate

Part 3

16 B   17 A   18 C   19 D   20 C

Part 4

21 B   22 E   23 H   24 A   25 C   26 B   27 A   28 F
29 E   30 C

Transcript	*This is the Cambridge English: Proficiency, Test One.*
	I am going to give you the instructions for this test. I shall introduce each part of the test and give you time to look at the questions.
	At the start of each piece, you will hear this sound:
	tone
	You will hear each piece twice.
	Remember, while you are listening, write your answers on the question paper. You will have five minutes at the end of the test to copy your answers onto the separate answer sheet.
	There will now be a pause. Please ask any questions now, because you must not speak during the test.
	[pause]
PART 1	*Now open your question paper and look at Part One.*
	[pause]
	You will hear three different extracts. For questions 1 to 6, choose the answer (A, B or C) which fits best according to what you hear. There are two questions for each extract.
Extract 1	[pause]
	tone
Emily:	So James, what's happening with the cracks in the ceiling of the blue salon?
James:	Well the last restoration of this ceiling took place 65 years ago and the team are having a hard time removing that paint job. People didn't seem to understand at the time that reversibility is a core principle of restoration work.
Emily:	Right. Nothing that's done should be too permanent.
James:	Yeah – in case a better method for restoration comes along. But they're getting there. Anyway, that's great news that you were able to buy back the original dining table, Emily.
Emily:	Yeah, thanks. Do you know it was one of the first pieces to be sold on after the palace was looted during the English civil war? The detective work involved in tracking all the

documentation was a pain – it took months, but it paid off in the end. The table was finally discovered in a private house in Australia. And luckily two donors came forward with the money or it would have blown our entire budget.

[pause]

tone

[The recording is repeated]

Extract 2   [pause]

tone

Man: What are the gelada monkeys doing that other primates don't, because I thought they all communicate vocally in some way?

Woman: They definitely do. But the issue for scientists has been – if you're thinking about where language came from – that most primate vocalisations are quite simple and flat, sort of, monosyllabic grunts. And if you look at what humans do when we communicate, it's nothing like that. So we make these long strings of really complicated sounds with ups and downs and loud parts and high parts. So scientists started to actually look elsewhere for possible precursors to human speech. And one thing they've been looking at is this facial movement that most primates do, including geladas, called lip-smacking. So this is a gesture that they perform in kind of friendly interactions between individuals – they're moving their mouth very quickly, sort of rapidly opening and closing their mouth. But in the case of these particular monkeys they actually vocalise while lip-smacking, and this produces a kind of undulation in the sound, which we call a wobble. And it's the pattern of intervals between the wobbles that reflects our own speech.

[pause]

tone

[The recording is repeated]

Extract 3   [pause]

tone

Man: How do you think journalism has changed over the years?

Woman: Technology changes things. It shouldn't affect the content, but it does eventually. So for example, the first impressions of anything – shocking, surprising, enlightening – are often inaccurate. But when stuff's going out live, both sound and pictures, which is increasingly what's expected, you don't have time to judge, ask why, know if something's staged or false, or it's misleading and insignificant, so there's more shaky information around now.

Then there's the internet. The bulk hits on news sites are people reading five headlines. It takes them fifteen seconds. They don't read further, unless it's something that pulls them in. Whereas with a newspaper, you sit through it, whether you're really interested or not. News used to be like a plateful of food, and you had to plough your way through everything you were given. Nowadays it's self-service on the internet. You've got a buffet of information, and most people just eat the chips and pudding. And those are sport and celebs. The rest of it – unrest in a foreign country, social complexities at home – are the bits which aren't actually very palatable.

[pause]

tone

[The recording is repeated]

[pause]

That is the end of Part One.

Test 1 Key

Now turn to Part Two.

[pause]

PART 2 *You will hear part of a lecture about an architect called Josh Keysall, who became famous for designing environmentally friendly houses known as Earthpods. For questions 7 to 15, complete the sentences with a word or short phrase.*

You now have forty-five seconds in which to look at Part Two.

[pause]

tone

I want to start this talk on alternative house design by telling you a little about a man called Josh Keysall, who has been a proponent of what he refers to as 'radically successful living' for many years. Keysall was born in Australia and studied architecture at the University of Melbourne. During his course he started to get interested in ways of using recycled materials for building.

After graduating in 1982, he followed up this interest. And very soon he had a moment of inspiration which has influenced his entire career. He realised that if he took discarded objects and filled them with dirt, he could create something that acted as effective insulation, keeping the inside of buildings cool in summer and warm in winter without the need to use dangerous or expensive materials such as spray foam for this purpose.

Keysall then started to use this technique to build houses, which he called 'Earthpods'. These are all built from things which would otherwise be thrown away. So, for example, in the first house he built, he constructed the walls by collecting together old cans, and wiring them together to act as bricks. Later Keysall used other materials such as sandbags. Soon he was building and selling his experimental homes, at the same time continuing to develop his techniques.

Keysall describes his Earthpods as 'passive solar buildings' in the way they function to regulate temperature. Apparently the thick walls of the houses absorb heat from the sun during the day when the weather is warm, and then slowly release it at night and during colder seasons, so they act as storage heaters. This is quite different from using conventional fossil fuels such as oil or gas for central heating as it is a sustainable system with no harmful by-products.

Keysall is proud of his buildings' green credentials. He says that his Earthpods are 'off the grid', meaning they've got no power lines coming in and no energy being used, but he says they're still extremely comfortable to live in.

At first he only built Earthpods in Australia, but soon people in other countries got interested in what he was doing. In Europe, the first Earthpod was built in a small village in Switzerland in 1987 and was modified to cope with the weather conditions there. It was originally a community centre, and was adapted for use as a hotel for tourists visiting the region.

As well as having to consider local conditions, Keysall also has to bear other factors in mind. In Belgium, he had planned to build an Earthpod out of car tyres. But this was not allowed because of the risk of contamination from the toxic metals like lead and zinc they contained, so for that project he had to use glass bottles instead.

In the UK, Keysall recently got planning permission to build sixteen Earthpod homes in a semi-rural area popular with public sector workers such as nurses and teachers. The plans for the project had to include safeguarding the habitat of lizards which were already living wild in the area.

However, although Keysall has always stressed the experimental nature of his buildings, some people found the designs unattractive, and they didn't always perform as promised. Disillusioned buyers started to file lawsuits and claims over leaking roofs and other problems. After a year-long dispute with several clients, Keysall was stripped of his professional licence in 2006 and his Earthpods were declared unsafe and illegal.

Faced with the end of his career, Keysall agreed to follow the required building codes, though not without protest. And though he chafed at not being able to experiment freely any more, Keysall got his architect's licence back and resumed building Earthpods. The documentary *Trash Pirate* recounts Keysall's struggle with the law and glorifies his life and work, and he is presented in the film as a green hero, a rebel whose concern over the environment was ahead of his time and is now vindicated.

[pause]

Now you will hear Part Two again.

tone

[The recording is repeated]

[pause]

That is the end of Part Two.

Now turn to Part Three.

[pause]

PART 3   *You will hear part of an interview in which two academics, Julia Ford and Stuart Cameron, discuss human memory. For questions 16 to 20, choose the answer (A, B, C or D) which fits best according to what you hear.*

You now have one minute in which to look at Part Three.

[pause]

tone

Interviewer: Hello and welcome to 'Mind to mind'. Today, my guests are Professors Julia Ford and Stuart Cameron, who are researching human memory. Julia, tell us about your work.

Julia: Well basically we're investigating the relationship between individual memory and shared memory, or social memory, and particularly we're looking at how reliable our memory is when it's shared. So memory researchers have mostly focused on individuals remembering alone, but in everyday life we probably as often remember with other people, with our family, our friends, and the people we work with. In cognitive psychology, memory researchers have been very worried about the influence of other people on our memories and assessing that.

Stuart: They worry that we're going to influence or infect one another's memories, particularly in the forensic setting, like if someone's a witness to a crime, and that's understandable because we don't want people who are giving testimony, for instance, to report things that they didn't experience, that they just picked up from other people.

Julia: But even so, you know, we don't think that worry necessarily has to extend to all the kinds of memory that we use and when we look at our everyday interactions it's actually helpful when we look to other people to help us remember.

Interviewer: Stuart, you've observed many older couples telling their stories and performing various memory tasks. What did you find?

Stuart: It was quite interesting because I was quite ideological in a way about the research, and I thought we would definitely see that everybody collaborated really well, and showed strong benefits of socially shared remembering. And in fact we didn't see that. What was really interesting was that some couples collaborated really effectively and performed much better when they were together than when they were apart, and other couples disrupted each other and didn't remember together effectively, at least on certain tasks. So these anomalies became the thing to explain and what I did was look at the processes that occurred while they discussed and while they shared remembering. So we recorded the conversations, and we coded each phrase that was

131

said for what it contained, and we looked for what kinds of ways of interacting with each other predicted memory performance.

Julia: And we found when they were sharing memories that some couples could cue each other really effectively in quite novel and idiosyncratic ways, so sometimes they would say "I know about tools, you know about clothes …"

Stuart: or, "you remember the first half and I'll remember the second half".

Julia: Right. So they'd split it up according to their understanding of each other's expertise. Although with tasks where one person was definitely the expert on the whole thing and the other wasn't, that really hampered successful collaboration, because the job tended to be all off-loaded onto one person. And so having a lot of shared experiences and a lot of shared history seemed to be helpful.

Stuart: Yeah. We saw more successful collaboration in tasks where their expertise was perceived as more shared and more distributed.

Julia: You know we're kind of unlike other animals in the extent to which it's part of our nature to rely on objects, technologies and the social world as well. Of course we're always in danger of losing things, of our technologies being destroyed, or you know losing touch with other people. We are kind of hostage to fortune compared to other animals, but that's just how we work.

Interviewer: And finally, a question for both of you: there's also the possibility that our brains are changing the way they operate, the way the memory works. Could that be a problem?

Stuart: It can be a problem, absolutely. I mean from a scientific and philosophical point of view I s'pose it's more immediately just fascinating to try and observe cultural changes in the kinds of technologies and objects that people have access to, and ignore the need for hard facts.

Julia: I'm certainly interested in the social nature of memory from the time that we started to draw paintings on the walls of caves, and I know Stuart is investigating our contemporary reliance on artefacts, technologies and so on.

Stuart: Yes, although it's a controversial theory, the role of civilisation is embedded in our view. It means over time and in different places and contexts human memory actually changes, not just its support but in its nature as well.

[pause]

Now you will hear Part Three again.

tone

[The recording is repeated]

[pause]

That is the end of Part Three.

Now turn to Part Four.

[pause]

PART 4 *Part Four consists of two tasks. You will hear five short extracts in which university students are talking about the profession they are training for. Look at Task One. For questions 21 to 25, choose from the list (A to H) how each speaker feels about their course. Now look at Task Two. For questions 26 to 30, choose from the list (A to H) what each speaker says about future prospects for those on the course. While you listen you must complete both tasks. You now have forty-five seconds in which to look at Part Four.*

[pause]

tone

Speaker One Medicine's been one of the most in-demand subjects for ages now, but a medical course is no picnic. Anyway, they say your performance after graduation counts for more than how you do in your studies. You need to specialise, and then it's your references, plus the general regard for you as a doctor, plus what you've published, that'll get you the post, or not, as the case may be. And if I slog to gain the theoretical knowledge, but don't keep abreast of things later in the course when I'm out on the wards, then I can forget about becoming a doctor.

[pause]

Speaker Two Studying Law's an experience that only other students of Law will appreciate. We're all agreed that we're finding it highly competitive and we're weighed down with reading stuff like case reports. They have these codes on them, which seem baffling, but with a bit of lateral thinking I've deciphered them, and since then, using them's been a breeze! Some people on the course are from families with a history of law practitioners, so they've got the assurance of a ready position awaiting them, with established networks. And though there are hundreds of law firms on the lookout for trainees, there's no guarantee of getting to be a mover and shaker in court. I've heard the greatest scope is in areas like international and cyber law.

[pause]

Speaker Three I was told, with the variety of topics in computers, there's a place for everyone. Apparently, the days when only mathematical geniuses made a mark in the field are gone, but the course is getting some people down – it's very much a 'same size fits all' approach and some people are struggling. I'm managing to stay ahead of the game though. Finding a job's not supposed to be difficult, though you can get lost among the millions who are mere cogs in the wheel of a huge corporation. We've been warned it won't be lucrative unless we carve out a niche area of expertise for ourselves, so we're not expecting our studies to bear fruit immediately or anything.

[pause]

Speaker Four Management courses became rather too popular some time ago, resulting in a throng of graduates who exceeded the demand of the market. It takes more than just perspiration to climb the corporate ladder, but I'm now prepared for that. A manager has to be a people person in order to meet the needs of the situation, and this adaptability is wanting in many otherwise high achievers. My course director told us he couldn't assure us we'd get an attractive salary package by the end of it but we would be thinking differently. The big picture of management is gradually unfolding and it's gruelling trying to get the hang of it, but fulfilling at the same time.

[pause]

Speaker Five I've realised that education isn't just about picking up practical stuff so I can sell myself on the job market. After signing up to study language and linguistics I've gained a handle on other stuff and insights into the diversity of life way beyond what you'd think. It's taking a while to cotton onto how to manage my study time and all that, but I'm getting there. Graduates tend to find employment relatively easily if they're not too fussy what area they work in, but if you actually want to make a career in linguistics the odds are pretty long. Anyway, I'm hoping to carry on to do postgraduate work, then I'll see.

[pause]

Now you will hear Part Four again.

tone

[The recording is repeated]

[pause]

That is the end of Part Four.

There will now be a pause of five minutes for you to copy your answers onto the separate answer sheet. Be sure to follow the numbering of all the questions. I shall remind you when there is one minute left, so that you are sure to finish in time.

[Teacher, pause the recording here for five minutes. Remind your students when they have one minute left.]

That is the end of the test. Please stop now. Your supervisor will now collect all the question papers and answer sheets.

Test 2 Key

Reading and Use of English (1 hour 30 minutes)

Part 1

1 C   2 A   3 B   4 D   5 A   6 B   7 D   8 B

Part 2

9 beyond   10 longer   11 in   12 making   13 result
14 other   15 like   16 all

Part 3

17 revelations   18 revolutionise / revolutionize   19 depths   20 comparatively
21 findings   22 significantly   23 emissions   24 endangered

Part 4

25 dislike of commuting | Sam would never have
26 showed/gave no sign | of nervousness
27 had every confidence | (that) his team was/were able
28 has been growth | in the number/numbers of
29 of the difficulties | (that are) involved in using
30 has been put off | until

Part 5

31 A   32 B   33 D   34 A   35 B   36 D

Part 6

37 B   38 A   39 D   40 G   41 H   42 C   43 F

Part 7

44 C   45 E   46 D   47 B   48 D   49 A   50 A   51 E
52 B   53 C

Writing (1 hour 30 minutes)

Briefing Document

Question 1

Content

Essay must refer to and evaluate the following points:
• some people can only relax at home
• at home they can reflect on the day's events
• we escape to public places where we can socialise and be ourselves
• home is a place where people express their personalities
• writer's own ideas on topic.

Question 5a

Content
Essay must:
- describe the role of the pearl earrings in Griet's story
- explain the way the earrings contribute to her losing her position in the house.

Answers must make reference to the content of the book. The following references may be contained in the candidate's answer:
- *Catharina's jewellery box, the pearl necklace and earrings as her property, which her husband requires her to lend to his models*
- *Catharina's mistrust of Griet and her jealousy about her role as the only other person regularly allowed in the studio*
- *Griet's comment, 'I have always wanted to wear pearls but knowing that a maid cannot wear such things (or a butcher's wife either),*
- *her appreciation/understanding that they are the one thing that will complete the picture of her and that will mean her ruin, because Catharina is bound to find out*
- *her reluctance and the pain she undergoes to wear them*
- *the significance of the earrings in Vermeer's will and what she decides to do with them (immediately sells them)*
- *earrings may be considered as symbolic of wealth, status, beauty, pain and conflict (numerous examples, e.g. piercing and wearing the earrings; symbolic of inner turmoil for Griet and open conflict with Catharina).*

Range
Language for:
- describing
- narrating
- explaining
- evaluating.

Appropriacy of register and format
Register consistently appropriate for essay for class tutor.

Organisation and cohesion
Well organised and paragraphed, with adequate use of linking.

Target reader
Would understand:
- the significance of the pearl earrings in Griet's story
- the way in which they contribute to Griet losing her position in the Vermeer household.

Question 5b

Content
Article must consider the importance of money in the relationship between John Law and Anna Moore and explain why the article about this novel should be included in the series.

Answers must make reference to the content of the book. The following references may be contained in the candidate's answer:

- paper currency and coins no longer in use, financial transactions governed by Soft Gold
- relationship starts out with Anna's investigation into John Law's financial affairs
- Anna is intrigued by John Law's motives for fraud
- her interest develops into attraction and obsession
- issue of trust as a result of her investigation into his tax affairs
- meets family, gets to know Anneli and Nathan, understands their vulnerability (Nathan is diabetic, can break the code, JL has made his money partly for the sake of his son)
- Anna's mother asks her to get JL to pay off sister Martha's debts
- the impression JL's wealth makes on Anna on her first visit to his house at Erith Reach.

Range
Language for:
- describing
- narrating
- explaining
- evaluating/recommending.

Appropriacy of register and format
Register consistently appropriate for an article in an English-language magazine.

Organisation and cohesion
- clearly organised ideas
- suitable introduction and conclusion.

Target reader
Would be interested and:
- understand the role played by money in the relationship between John Law and Anna Moore
- know why the candidate thought that the article on the novel would be worth including in the series.

Listening (approximately 40 minutes)

Part 1

1 A 2 B 3 B 4 A 5 B 6 A

Part 2

7 clay 8 seeds 9 crocodiles 10 mines 11 leaves 12 pumps
13 fences 14 island 15 legislation

Part 3

16 C 17 B 18 D 19 A 20 C

Part 4

21 E 22 G 23 H 24 F 25 A 26 G 27 A 28 E
29 D 30 C

Transcript

This is the Cambridge English: Proficiency, Test 2.

I am going to give you the instructions for this test. I shall introduce each part of the test and give you time to look at the questions.

At the start of each piece, you will hear this sound:

tone

You will hear each piece twice.

Remember, while you are listening, write your answers on the question paper. You will have five minutes at the end of the test to copy your answers onto the separate answer sheet.

There will now be a pause. Please ask any questions now, because you must not speak during the test.

[pause]

PART 1

Now open your question paper and look at Part One.

[pause]

You will hear three different extracts. For questions 1 to 6, choose the answer (A, B or C) which fits best according to what you hear. There are two questions for each extract.

Extract 1

[pause]

tone

All of you are graduating with a degree in science. So what is science? Some people say that it's about discovering facts and truths about the natural world. In my own field, which is climate science, it's not uncommon to hear about scientific debates, uncertainties and scepticism. Indeed, repeated questioning and testing of our understanding is a fundamental part of all science.

However, this does not mean that every claim about climate change published in a newspaper or on the web is correct. Science is about building up and evaluating the whole body of evidence on a phenomenon. It is based on reproducible observations and experiments. Science is not about selecting a few pieces of data that support an idea and ignoring the rest. Selective misuse of small amounts of data or taking observations out of context to support an agenda is not science.

Given this, I'm sure I don't need to tell you the most important thing that you've learned as part of your degree is not the facts that you've learned but the scientific method, the skills to collect, analyse and evaluate data. Value and build on those skills.

[pause]

tone

[The recording is repeated]

Extract 2

[pause]

tone

Man: Now today there are a few human beings who, for biological reasons, cannot forget, which sounds like a blessing. They certainly do remember where they parked their car in a shopping mall. But it turns out that they have tremendous difficulties in acting in time, in deciding in time, because they remember all their bad, failed decisions in the past, and therefore hesitate to make a decision in the present. Because they're forever tethered to the past, they can't act, they can't stay put in the present, and they can't imagine the future.

Woman: So what's the difference between human memory and computer memory, or storage?

Man: Computer storage is the capturing of a flow of bits and the retrieval of a flow of bits. It is decontextualised. It is taken out of its original context. We can only guess in what context, in what situation, it was said, or done, or captured. Human memory, in contrast, is capable of putting things in perspective, of linking events with other events and experiences, of adding context and feeling to it, of reconstructing memory to fit better our own later understanding of what happened.

[pause]

tone

[The recording is repeated]

Extract 3 [pause]

tone

Man: Do you think e-books will eventually replace paper ones?

Woman: I don't know. There's something about the experience of having a book that's special, isn't there, the feel of it, the cover, all that. You can scribble in it or even spill your coffee on it and it's not the end of the world. And if it's well-thumbed rather than being pristine, I actually prefer it that way.

Man: Not having to fill up your hand luggage with great heavy tomes when you're getting a flight abroad is a real advantage, though. And you don't have books gathering dust all over the place at home either. But you can't rifle through the pages in the same way with an electronic device.

Woman: Mm. It's interesting the way technology's trying to replicate some of that experience of books – like turning a page.

Man: I think the really interesting thing is how they'll affect newspapers. Maybe if more people subscribe to read the news online it'll give the newspaper industry a boost, or maybe it's really defunct. I mean, even quality papers are having a difficult time of it at the moment.

[pause]

tone

[The recording is repeated]

[pause]

That is the end of Part One.

Now turn to Part Two.

[pause]

PART 2   *You will hear a student called Tom giving a presentation about non-native species of animals in Australia, and the problems they cause. For questions 7 to 15, complete the sentences with a word or short phrase.*

You now have forty-five seconds in which to look at Part Two.

[pause]

tone

I'm going to talk about some of the new species of animals that have been introduced into Australia, and the problems they've caused. Native animals like the kangaroo lived in Australia for millions of years. But when the Europeans came to settle there in the eighteenth century, they brought new animals with them, and these sometimes had a serious effect on the local ecosystems.

One of the introduced species that caused most harm was the rabbit. They were introduced in the nineteenth century as food and kept in cages, but they soon escaped and took over almost the entire country. The only areas where they're still relatively scarce is where the ground consists of clay, as they like to have soft ground or sand to dig their burrows in. This means they're happy to live in deserts as well as farming land.

These rabbits have had a huge impact on native Australian species as they compete with them for food. The rabbits eat the bark from young trees, which kills the trees, and they also consume vast quantities of young plants, destroying them before they can produce the seeds that native birds depend on for their food.

One way you can deal with a harmful species such as the rabbit is to find another species that preys on it. But this doesn't always work out. A famous example is the case of the cane toad. This was deliberately introduced into Australia so that it would destroy small beetles that were harming the sugar-cane crop. Well, it turned out that the cane toad wasn't particularly good at killing the beetles, but it was highly poisonous to other creatures – it could even be fatal to crocodiles. Because it has no predators, the cane toad has spread widely and become a major pest throughout large parts of Australia, and it's had serious effects on the biodiversity of these regions. Biologists are trying hard to stop the spread of the toads, but so far they've been unsuccessful.

One animal that you wouldn't expect to find in Australia is the camel. It's certainly not native to Australia, but in fact it's estimated that there are more than a million camels there. They were first introduced in the nineteenth century as a way of providing transportation in the sandy deserts of central Australia. They were kept on farms and used for riding, and they also proved invaluable as beasts of burden, supplying necessary goods to the mines way out in the Australian outback. But once other forms of transportation arrived, the camels were released into the wild where they bred and multiplied, feeding on a wide range of vegetation and having a huge impact on the life cycle of plants. They're particularly attracted by apricot trees, and strip the branches in search of the leaves, which means the tree's unable to produce flowers or fruits. As well as affecting the environment, wild camels in Australia may do damage of other sorts. In times of drought they've been known to come into remote villages in search of water and wreck the pumps there. Many of these communities are very poor, and the damage done by camels in this way can be hard to repair.

So what can be done to prevent invasive species from spreading further in Australia? One solution is to deliberately introduce diseases to wipe out a particular species. This was attempted with rabbits, and it was initially successful, but eventually the rabbits developed resistance to the disease. Attempts to build fences to contain the spread of invasive species can only work on a small scale due to the high cost of building and maintaining them. Shooting or trapping can be used, but the problem's too big for these to be effective methods. In fact, the only place where invasive species have been fully eradicated is an island and it seems the mainland is just too huge for eradication to be possible in spite of all the problems this causes the owners of farms there.

But the experts haven't given up. The consensus is that broad efforts to control large areas of the country will be useless – instead targets have to be limited, so that the work's done a little at a time. And, of course, the country imposes legislation so that further introduction, deliberate or accidental, of potentially invasive species can be controlled. So perhaps there's hope that in the future the problem will begin to go away.

[pause]

Now you will hear Part Two again.

tone

[The recording is repeated]

[pause]

That is the end of Part Two.

Now turn to Part Three.

[pause]

PART 3   *You will hear part of an interview with two British architects, Malcolm Fletcher and Alison Brooks, about the design of new low-cost housing. For questions 16 to 20, choose the answer (A, B, C or D) which fits best according to what you hear.*

You now have one minute in which to look at Part Three.

[pause]

tone

Interviewer: Welcome to today's programme on current issues. Today I'd like to welcome two architects, Malcolm Fletcher and Alison Brooks, who both specialise in domestic architecture. So, starting with you Alison … What's your reaction to the government's plans to build houses on what in the UK are classified as greenfield sites – sites that are currently in their natural state, or used as farmland?

Alison: Well I think it's inevitable really. There'll be a lot of opposition to it from groups who want to protect the countryside from any development. It's understandable, but Britain is a small crowded country and you have to be realistic. People need homes, don't they, Malcolm?

Malcolm: Yes, if you take some of our older cities, like Bath, or York, or Edinburgh – they were built on what were originally greenfield sites, but no one's suggesting that we pull them down. Because people like those buildings. Compared to them, houses that have been built in recent years are unimaginative, to say the least.

Interviewer: So how can we ever get out of this situation, break the mould? Malcolm?

Malcolm: There are individual cases where an architect's designed something different, and better. For example there's a small housing development in Essex called Newhall. The key to the innovative design of these houses seems to have been the fact that the people who the land previously belonged to didn't just take as much money as they could and then lose interest. Before they agreed to sell the land, they set conditions which the architect and builders had to meet in order to ensure that the local people would benefit as much as possible from the development.

Alison: The commission for the development was actually won by an architect called Margaret Gibbs. I went there recently. There are about eighty houses altogether. They're quite an unusual shape, and they're made of black timber and yellowish-coloured brick. They're quite striking just because they look different, and I must say that although I like the visual aspect of her design myself and the reference they make to traditional architecture, they're not everybody's cup of tea.

Malcolm: I think what really distinguishes them from most recent housing developments in this country is that the architect really has paid attention to details which affect the quality of life of the people living in them. And like the way that by using a clever system of

141

timber cassettes she avoided the need to have timber beams supporting the roof. That means that instead of being wasted, the roof space became available for use. Often young couples have to move to a bigger house when they have children, but in Gibbs's houses they can use the roof space as an extra bedroom.

Alison: But in terms of total area, they're the same as a conventional plot for small houses. But whereas conventional developers build long thin houses, Gibbs has made hers almost square. So her hall and stairs aren't just narrow strips – she calls them 'an active, social space' which is more central to the plan.

Interviewer: What are the Essex houses like outside? What about the surrounding space?

Malcolm: Well Margaret Gibbs has given her houses patios and roof decks and porches, but not gardens, so they aren't suitable for horticulturists. But then not everyone wants to tend the apron of green that you get with conventional new houses. And there are playing fields and other public green spaces nearby anyway.

Alison: Yes. And Gibbs says she wanted to make the street itself into an extension of the living space. So the balconies and the studies face the street and people who work from home don't feel isolated. She wanted to change the suburban street from a desolate place into a little working community.

Interviewer: So to round up then, how do Margaret Gibbs's new houses match up to those of Britain's older cities? Are they just as aesthetically pleasing as houses in Bristol or Bath for example?

Alison: They're very different, and they won't please everyone. But I don't think it's helpful to talk about beauty actually. It's so subjective.

Malcolm: Yes. When people talk about a building being 'beautiful' or 'stylish', they usually mean that it matches their own personal tastes. So it's not a very useful criterion for assessing architecture. Where we should be going in future I think, is looking at the extent to which houses enhance people's quality of life and function well.

Interviewer: Right ... well ... Malcolm Fletcher and Alison Brooks – thank you.

[pause]

Now you will hear Part Three again.

tone

[The recording is repeated]

[pause]

That is the end of Part Three.

Now turn to Part Four.

[pause]

PART 4

Part Four consists of two tasks.
You will hear five short extracts in which people talk about academic conferences they have attended. Look at Task One. For questions 21 to 25, choose from the list (A to H) the reason each speaker gives for wanting to attend an academic conference. Now look at Task Two. For questions 26 to 30, choose from the list (A to H) how each speaker felt about the first presenter. While you listen you must complete both tasks.

You now have forty-five seconds in which to look at Part Four.

[pause]

tone

Speaker One   I was looking forward to the conference. I'm doing research into kidney function and while I get on really well with the people in the clinic, and I'm getting some interesting data, there are some knotty areas where I'd really appreciate the chance to exchange ideas with another specialist. I also wanted to get a feel for how these things work before I give my own paper next year. I nearly left after the first presentation though. That was by Mark Bradley, about developments in kidney transplants, and although the research he described was interesting, I knew the people who'd done it, and I was aware that he misreported some of the results, which was alarming.

[pause]

Speaker Two   The first speaker had everyone in stitches from the start, although personally I didn't see the funny side. He was talking about funding for the arts, and you'd expect some sort of argument, wouldn't you, or at least a position, but all we got was a string of examples and anecdotes – well told, but that's not the point. Anyway, things got better after that and I'm glad I went. Having taught twelve weeks without a break, and then the summer school, I was ready for some R and R, and when they published the conference details, the combination of the location and the travel grant clinched it for me. Shame my buddies couldn't make it, but never mind.

[pause]

Speaker Three   The opening presentation was something else. Repeating his key points could have been quite an effective way for the speaker to get his message across, but I began to feel that either he hadn't had a proper run through or he didn't know his stuff, and as the uhming and ahing went on, we didn't know where to look. But I wasn't there for that. I had a problem to solve. Over the years I've written lots of teaching material and I'd like to see it in print, maybe get a holiday with the proceeds. But I didn't know who to go to. And then I realised there'd be book exhibition stands and representatives at the conference. Problem solved.

[pause]

Speaker Four   In academia, I know the only way to get ahead is to get published. Now I'm not the most focused of people, and I always want to just follow a few more research leads, but a colleague advised me that if I had to write my material up so it was ready to give at a conference, that'd provide me with a clear objective. Well, I managed to do that, and it got accepted. And I really enjoyed the conference. The opening speaker charmed everyone with his light-hearted accounts of his early career as a librarian, and the exaggerated claims made for new classification systems. He had a substantial amount of experience but he didn't labour it.

[pause]

Speaker Five   Professionally I was feeling a little down. Friends told me I needed a vacation, but I had plenty of drive. It was just that for my own sake I needed to get up to speed with innovations in the field, and I decided attending a conference was a quick fix. Anyway, the opening presenter's methodology and his analytical approach, I could buy – lots of detail, that all made sense. But his findings didn't all quite hack it for me, and some of the claims he made in his conclusion were a bit dubious as a result. But at least it was original stuff, I suppose, which is more than can be said for some of the papers I heard.

[pause]

Now you will hear Part Four again.

tone

[The recording is repeated]

[pause]

That is the end of Part Four.

There will now be a pause of five minutes for you to copy your answers onto the separate answer sheet. Be sure to follow the numbering of all the questions. I shall remind you when there is one minute left, so that you are sure to finish in time.

[Teacher, pause the recording here for five minutes. Remind your students when they have one minute left.]

That is the end of the test. Please stop now. Your supervisor will now collect all the question papers and answer sheets.

Test 3 Key

Reading and Use of English (1 hour 30 minutes)

Part 1

1 C   2 C   3 B   4 D   5 A   6 A   7 D   8 C

Part 2

9 every   10 worst   11 from   12 reason   13 goes
14 more   15 use   16 while

Part 3

17 democratised/democratized   18 encountered   19 instinctively
20 outstanding   21 revolutionary   22 unconditionally   23 inner   24 embedded

Part 4

25 think you will/you'll find (that) | few road atlases
26 were under/had no | obligation (whatsoever) to make
27 couldn't/could not be bothered | to put
28 was nothing (that) Tom | could do except
29 sudden decision to retire | came as a surprise
30 has no intention | of (ever) climbing

Part 5

31 C   32 B   33 B   34 A   35 A   36 B

Part 6

37 B   38 F   39 H   40 G   41 A   42 C   43 E

Part 7

44 A   45 C   46 E   47 D   48 B   49 C   50 D   51 E   52 C   53 B

Writing (1 hour 30 minutes)

Briefing Document

Question 1

Content
Essay must refer to and evaluate the following points:
• formal clothes can create a feeling of distance between people
• we feel reassured by professional people who dress formally
• uniforms may intimidate some people
• formal dress is an integral part of national occasions
• writer's own ideas on topic.

Question 5a

Content
- Consideration of the approach to justice in Okonkwo's clan
- Assessment of the impact of that approach on people's lives

Range
Language of description and assessment

Appropriacy of register and format
Format for a review

Organisation and cohesion
Well organised in paragraphs

Target reader
Would be clearly informed about the novel

Question 5b

Content
Report should include:
A description of the way the characters respond to the Inspector's questions
An evaluation of what this reveals about their personalities

Range
Language of description, evaluation and comparison

Appropriacy of register and format
Report format, possibly with clear section headings
Register consistently appropriate for relationship between writer and drama group

Organisation and cohesion
Well-structured report with clear sections
Presentation of ideas in well-organised prose
Adequate use of linking and paragraphing

Target reader
Would be informed about the attitudes of the four members of the family and the contrast between the parents and children

Listening (approximately 40 minutes)

Part 1

1 B   2 C   3 C   4 C   5 A   6 B

Part 2

7 martial arts   8 mind   9 experiment   10 equally matched   11 referee
12 visibility   13 dominance (and) aggression   14 rivals   15 status

Part 3

16 B   17 C   18 D   19 A   20 B

Part 4

21 D   22 G   23 E   24 A   25 F   26 A   27 F
28 C   29 H   30 G

Transcript	*This is the Cambridge English: Proficiency, Test Three.*
	I am going to give you the instructions for this test. I shall introduce each part of the test and give you time to look at the questions. At the start of each piece, you will hear this sound:
	tone
	You will hear each piece twice. Remember, while you are listening, write your answers on the question paper. You will have five minutes at the end of the test to copy your answers onto the separate answer sheet.
	There will now be a pause. Please ask any questions now, because you must not speak during the test.
	[pause]
PART 1	*Now open your question paper and look at Part One.*
	[pause]
	You will hear three different extracts. For questions 1 to 6, choose the answer (A, B or C) which fits best according to what you hear. There are two questions for each extract.
Extract 1	[pause]
	tone
	Am I supposed to start worrying about hedgehogs, because their numbers are decreasing here in Britain? I don't know how they know this – it's like the estimate of the number of cats in the USA. I recall someone commenting that the man who counted the cats had a terrible time and said he wouldn't want to do it again. But whether the hedgehogs matter … I only knew one personally; it showed up in our garden and had to be repatriated to the local park in a cat basket. It left an uncounted number of fleas in it, which I don't suppose are an endangered species.
	I know we worry about badgers and the cattle that they may or may not contaminate, and about declining coral creatures. And famished polar bears. But how many things are we supposed to take sides on? Do we have to worry about things we can't affect? Take the plans to close my local hospital – do politicians and business leaders really notice what the public think about things like this, and act accordingly? Well maybe, sometimes. There's a case for selective indignation. But I'm

not convinced about the hedgehogs.

[pause]

tone

[The recording is repeated.]

Extract 2 [pause]

tone

I always imagine life's goals as skyscrapers. The vast majority of people compete against each other trying to climb the stairs or cram into the elevators. But the fastest way to get to the top floor of a skyscraper isn't to climb the stairs or squeeze into the elevators. No. The fastest way to get onto the top floor of a skyscraper is to parachute down onto it from above!

It's about thinking big! Because here's the funny thing… when you shoot higher, you actually encounter less competition along the way, not more.

Don't get me wrong. I'm not a proponent of blind optimism. I'm actually a bit of a pessimist myself. But statistically, very few people shoot for massive goals. Everyone wants to be realistic. Well, there's some fascinating research around this topic, and it turns out that shooting for the massive goals isn't such a bad idea after all.

[pause]

tone

[The recording is repeated.]

Extract 3 [pause]

tone

Woman: How would you say you're different from other publishers?

Man: I've published work that may have taken a long time to get through more traditional companies. Where an editor didn't see its potential or wasn't prepared to go out on a limb. The industry tends to get stuck in a rut. We published a novel recently by a Swedish writer. She'd been to a few other publishers with it and they were all a bit concerned because it was actually quite quirky and they were expecting some sort of dark realistic Nordic crime novel. But we were prepared to accept that wasn't where she was going.

Woman: Do you think there's a classic 'editor type'?

Man: In capitalist economies there are market forces. People tend to go with trends. So when successful authors like J.K. Rowling and Dan Brown came onto the scene, editors were out looking for their clones. But we are talking big publishers here. When you look at small presses, they do interesting work regardless of who the editors are, because they don't have the same pressures. It's just that when companies get to a certain size and have shareholders, then they change.

[pause]

tone

[The recording is repeated.]

[pause]

That is the end of Part One.

Now turn to Part Two.

[pause]

PART 2 *You will hear a radio presenter called Tom Lee describing the psychological effects of the colour red on humans and animals. For questions 7 to 15, complete the sentences with a word or short phrase.*

You now have forty-five seconds in which to look at Part Two.

[pause]

tone

Hi. This is Tom Lee and in today's programme, I'd like to talk to you about the effects of the colour red. Imagine for a moment that you're watching something like a boxing match. Do you think that if one of the contestants wore red it would make any difference to who won the match? You'd probably say 'no', but at one British university, psychologists discovered that undergraduate students who were dressed in red scored higher in martial arts events than on other occasions when the same students were dressed in blue.

This is just the latest piece of research suggesting that exposure to certain colours can have a significant effect on how people think and act. People have always suspected that this might be true, but in the past this wasn't based on any solid research. However, evidence is now building on the way that the working of the mind is influenced by the colours we perceive through our eyes.

The powerful influence of colour on sporting success was first discovered a few years ago, when an evolutionary anthropologist called Ella Beecham was looking for a way to find out whether colours influence human behaviour. When she realised that those competing in certain Olympic events are told to wear blue or red outfits at random, she spotted an experiment which was effectively set up for her, rather like a business investment waiting to be seized upon.

When Beecham analysed the results of a series of wrestling matches, she found that the colour of the shirt influenced the outcome, with over half the bouts being won by the contestant in red. In bouts where contestants were equally matched, she found the proportion was even higher, instead of being roughly fifty-fifty, as would have been expected.

Beecham went on to claim that these differences may be accounted for, to some extent, by the positive inclination that the referee has towards red. She argues that this orientation is unconscious, but that it may have a measurable effect on the assessment of a contestant. She says that there is now good experimental evidence that red stimuli are perceived as dominant in such situations.

Beecham was also interested in whether red exerts its influence in team games. She looked at the possibility that higher or lower visibility, as a result of wearing different colours, affected the performance of team members playing on the same side in football. For example, she thought it could be beneficial for increased accuracy in passing, but she found no such effect. So that hypothesis was rejected.

Instead, most researchers now believe that red directly affects how the wearer of that colour is perceived. In the natural world, red is often used to signal dominance and aggression. And in the human world red is now used as a warning and a prohibition for motorists in cultures around the world.

One of the first scientists to explore the effect of red on animal behaviour was Nobel prizewinning ethologist Niko Tinbergen. Around fifty years ago, Tinbergen observed that every time a red postvan stationed itself on the other side of the window, the sticklebacks in his fish tank assumed a head-down position, something they would usually do only when confronting rivals. This wasn't the case with predators, who they would rather flee from.

Red is also a major influence on the behaviour of primates. The most ubiquitous monkey species are mandrills, and when they are in a situation where conflict is likely, the males assume red faces and rumps as a kind of status symbol. Where there are large colour differences, the paler male usually stands down, and so this acts as a means of managing the situation.

It could be that red is involved [*fade*]

[pause]

Now you will hear Part Two again.

tone

[The recording is repeated.]

[pause]

That is the end of Part Two.

Now turn to Part Three.

[pause]

PART 3   *You will hear a radio programme in which two people, Alison Kreel and David Walsh, who each run a food business, are discussing the premises they share. For questions 16 to 20, choose the answer (A, B, C or D) which fits best according to what you hear.*

You now have one minute in which to look at Part Three.

[pause]

tone

Interviewer: The old Siston building has now been renovated and my guests today are just a couple of the dynamic entrepreneurs who are busy cooking up new and exciting food products from the communal kitchens there: Alison Kreel of Kreel Soups and David Walsh from Sea Veg salads. Great to have you on the programme … Now tell me, is there any more room in the market for new quality food businesses? Some would say we've reached saturation point …

Alison: Not at all. That's what's so exciting – it seems people can't get enough of high quality food products.

David: Yeah but it's changing – customers are much more discerning than they used to be – they want to know how the food is produced, which was much less the case in the past.

Alison: And how it's sourced too. And you really need a strong brand identity to break into the market which isn't how it used to be – especially here in Brooklyn where there's such a strong food culture.

David: Yeah customers here really keep you on your toes!

Interviewer: I can believe that! …There's been a lot of investment put into the Siston building. Why do you think it's been so easy to get funding for projects like this?

David: It's a win-win situation. Iconic old buildings get a makeover and a new lease of life and young businesses get a kick start. I don't know how many of us would still be in work if we didn't have this opportunity – since the authorities started coming down hard on anyone trying to start a business from their own kitchen.

Interviewer Because all kitchens have to be state-certified?

David: Right. So I think investors understood that it's a way of keeping the entrepreneurial spirit alive – anyone could see that this project was a safe bet as there's huge demand for our kind of products. But you'd need serious money behind you to go it alone.

Alison: Yeah fifty thousand dollars minimum.

Interviewer: So I can see that it works in financial terms but what's it like sharing kitchen space?

Alison: I'd say there are more gains than losses. It's inspiring being around like-minded creative individuals. We kind of bounce off each other.

David: It does mean there's no thinking space though. But as a group we buy in bulk from suppliers which makes things cheaper.

Alison: And we're so close to all our main markets. And you know making soup, which is what

I'm involved in, is a messy business so what blew me away was the waterproof 'clean' room. Cleaning up used to take forever but now I can just hose everything down in a matter of minutes.

David: I think that's it. We're really lucky because the space has been so well thought out – everything's state-of-the-art.

Alison: So we're all able to work much more efficiently.

Interviewer: So has the moving into the new building changed the way you view your future?

Alison: For me – yes. I'm in a really good place now with a clear sense of direction which is to build up my customer base locally. Both from my own market stall and by supplying delis. It's also dawned on me that I should try out making smoothies in summer when demand for soup isn't that high. So my grand plans of opening my own chain of cafés nationwide are on hold for the moment!

Interviewer: I see. So what advice would you pass on to someone just starting out?

David: I probably should say do your homework – test out recipes on friends, get a job in a food market, talk to other food producers and learn from their mistakes, and of course make sure you can make a reasonable margin. Do you know what? Nothing beats just going ahead and doing it.

Alison: Otherwise it's easy to talk yourself out of the whole idea.

Interviewer   Well, I'm afraid that's all we [*fade*]

[pause]

Now you will hear Part Three again.

tone

[The recording is repeated.]

[pause]

That is the end of Part Three.

Now turn to Part Four.

[pause]

PART 4   *Part Four consists of two tasks. You will hear five short extracts in which people talk about studying abroad. Look at Task 1. For questions 21 to 25, choose from the list (A to H) the reason each speaker gives for wanting to study abroad. Now look at Task 2. For questions 26 to 30, choose from the list (A to H) how each speaker felt about their studies abroad. While you listen you must complete both tasks.*

You now have forty-five seconds in which to look at Part Four.

[pause]

tone

Speaker One   I was always very independent and I conquered my fear of foreign travel early on. When I went to study in Japan I did hit some problems like the lack of soundproofing of the dorms, but I discovered all kinds of other back-up from the Student Life centre and I was grateful for that. I wanted a new take on my field and to go somewhere I could experiment with lab cultures and new techniques for growing proteins, and also where I could maintain my linguistic skills. What I found surprising overall was the mono-ethnic nature of academic life, with relatively few students like me from overseas, but I already spoke excellent Japanese so it wasn't an issue for me.

[pause]

Speaker Two	I'm a person who normally dislikes change; I like to keep one set of friends and a routine. As a child I'd been tied to mom's apron strings, but by the time I was eighteen I decided that I'd had enough of that and going to college on the other side of the world was my way of dealing with it. My fees were paid but I wasn't sure I could support myself and it wasn't easy searching around for advice agencies. I'd thought it might be a bit of a shock living in a dorm, but it suited me down to the ground. And it's been quite an eye opener hearing what people think about my home country.

[pause]

Speaker Three	I was really looking forward to taking part in a task-based programme abroad. I knew that the basic focus in my subject, that's Cultural Studies, was no different from back home but it gave me the chance to experience an alternative mode of course delivery. In fact, though some of the modules were demanding, and I didn't do so well at first, I enjoyed the challenge. I was bowled over by the cosmopolitan nature of the campus. And although the timetable was full most days, there wasn't all that much follow-up work to do on our own, so I was free to make the most of the leisure facilities.

[pause]

Speaker Four	I discovered I'd been quite unrealistic about what I set out to do. When I applied for the study abroad programme, the fact that all the classes were taught in another language slowed me down like I was wearing lead boots and I hadn't expected so many out-of-class assignments. As well as that, I was surprised by how homesick I was for my family, so both these things were problems for me. But I'd wanted to study some place where university procedures were less bureaucratic, and at the time I was really curious about an alternative way of living. I wanted to immerse myself in that. I was also excited by the prospect of an internship, though I wasn't yet thinking about a career.

[pause]

Speaker Five	Although they were expensive, I had no worries about the tuition fees, thanks to a generous sponsor. When I applied I hadn't been sure whether I was taking on too much by opting for a year's law conversion course. It certainly delivered the goods as far as intellectual quality was concerned, and you were expected to step up to the plate in seminars and tutorials, but luckily it turned out that with self-discipline it was doable. I'd been keen to broaden my circle a bit, and I assumed it would be easy, but I was dependent on my host family for transport, so that clipped my wings a bit.

[pause]

Now you will hear Part Four again.

tone

[The recording is repeated.]

[pause]

That is the end of Part Four.

There will now be a pause of five minutes for you to copy your answers onto the separate answer sheet. Be sure to follow the numbering of all the questions. I shall remind you when there is one minute left, so that you are sure to finish in time.

[Teacher, pause the recording here for five minutes. Remind your students when they have one minute left.]

That is the end of the test. Please stop now. Your supervisor will now collect all the question papers and answer sheets.

Test 4 Key

Reading and Use of English (1 hour 30 minutes)

Part 1
1 D   2 C   3 C   4 A   5 C   6 D   7 B   8 A

Part 2
9 speaking   10 that / something   11 nor / neither   12 mind   13 long
14 but   15 think   16 given / with

Part 3
17 specifically   18 enumerated   19 reference   20 unimaginable
21 initiative(s)   22 pervasive   23 critically   24 shortcomings

Part 4
25 are Tom's chances | of
26 explanation has ever been given | for his decision
27 little prospect | of (him / his) being able
28 only time | will tell
29 make no | mention of
30 to the best | of his knowledge

Part 5
31 D   32 C   33 C   34 D   35 A   36 D

Part 6
37 F   38 G   39 A   40 H   41 B   42 D   43 E

Part 7
44 E   45 D   46 A   47 E   48 B   49 C   50 D   51 B
52 C   53 C

Writing (1 hour 30 minutes)

Briefing Document

Question 1

Content
Essay must refer to and evaluate the following points:
- we get pleasure from reminiscing with others about past events
- it is better to focus on the present rather than compare it with the past
- our memories contribute to our sense of identity
- our memories are unreliable and inconsistent
- writer's own ideas on topic.

Question 5a

Content
Description of the characters of both Bill and Josella
Comparison of the two characters and an evaluation of how their characters cause
them to respond in different ways

Range
Language of description
Language of comparison
Language of evaluation

Appropriacy of register and format
Essay style

Organisation and cohesion
Well paragraphed with appropriate links between the two characters

Target reader
Tutor would be informed about the characters of Bill and Josella and how the
differences in their characters caused them to react in different ways.

Question 5b

Content
Clear reference to chosen book
Recommendation of novel with clear focus on theme of loss of innocence

Range
Language of recommendation
Language of description
Language of narration

Appropriacy of register and format
Formal letter

Organisation and cohesion
Clear development of ideas with appropriate linking of paragraphs

Target reader
Would know whether novel would be suitable to be featured in literary journal

Listening (approximately 40 minutes)

Part 1

1 B   2 A   3 A   4 B   5 C   6 B

Part 2

7 geese   8 stopover   9 first officer   10 fuel   11 degree
12 vague desire   13 sense of calm   14 safari   15 antisocial hours

Part 3

16 B   17 C   18 D   19 B   20 A

Part 4

21 H   22 B   23 F   24 G   25 A   26 D   27 B
28 A   29 H   30 C

Transcript	*This is the Cambridge English: Proficiency, Test Four.*
	I am going to give you the instructions for this test. I shall introduce each part of the test and give you time to look at the questions. At the start of each piece, you will hear this sound:
	tone
	You will hear each piece twice. Remember, while you are listening, write your answers on the question paper. You will have five minutes at the end of the test to copy your answers onto the separate answer sheet.
	There will now be a pause. Please ask any questions now, because you must not speak during the test.
	[pause]
PART 1	*Now open your question paper and look at Part One.*
	[pause]
	You will hear three different extracts. For questions 1 to 6, choose the answer (A, B or C) which fits best according to what you hear. There are two questions for each extract.
Extract 1	[pause]
	tone
Woman:	Your adverts describe you as a small, family-owned business, but some people are claiming that you have considerable financial backing.
Man:	Well since my partner and I set up our business in 2006 we've operated totally independently. Yes, we're backed by an Indian company. That fact isn't difficult to find out with a few clicks of a mouse. But now we're self-financing and profitable.
	We had an ambition to make better-quality tea more available in the UK, and our growth appears to back up our belief that tea drinkers want something better than the slop they've been used to. So for those who're interested, we operate out of our own office in London, we now employ eight people and we're recruiting more as we speak. Every decision we've ever made has been made by us; no outside influence whatsoever. And, believe it or not, we don't have mega budgets to spend and quite frankly, we don't need them. We're thankful for our start-up backing but we're even more thankful for our independence. So, if anyone fancies a tea and some chat, then please pop down and visit us. You'll be very welcome.

[pause]

tone

[The recording is repeated.]

Extract 2 [pause]

tone

We're living in an age of systems in industrialised countries today. And the way that we work and we learn, the way that we communicate with each other, all these aspects of our lives are mediated by digital networks and systems. And why is that relevant for games? Because in a certain sense, games are the cultural form of systems. To play a game, to play a game against another player, is to push and pull the inputs and outputs of a system, to actually try something out, to play with the machinery of cause and effect. And in that sense, games have a special relationship to systems.

But I think that the games that let us play with each other in the most intimate way are board games. And maybe there's some part of our brains that really likes to be in a room with other people. From my own experience I certainly love playing board games, and if I think about the most fun that I have in general playing games, it's actually not with computer and video games, it's actually with playing old-fashioned board games.

[pause]

tone

[The recording is repeated.]

Extract 3 [pause]

tone

Man: About three years ago I made a discovery. Whether it's Mahatma Ghandi or Steve Jobs or Google, all the great leaders and organisations in the world, think, act and communicate in the exact same way. And it's the complete opposite from everyone else. These leaders and these organisations all think, act and communicate, from conviction, from their hearts. And if you talk about what you believe, you will act as a magnet to those who believe what you believe.

Why is it important to do this? Well, according to the theory of diffusion of innovations, the population's divided into groups. First, there's what's called the laggards – the ones who only buy ballpoint pens because shops no longer stock ink for fountain pens. Then there's the next group, who are a shade quicker to embrace new developments. Above them are what's known as the early adopters, and right at the top you have the innovators – and it's these two groups that matter in business terms. If they believe in what you're doing, the others will follow, and your product will take off.

[pause]

tone

[The recording is repeated.]

[pause]

That is the end of Part One.

Now turn to Part Two.

[pause]

PART 2 *You will hear an airline pilot called Rebecca Martin talking on the radio about a typical day in her job. For questions 7 to 15, complete the sentences with a word or short phrase.*

You now have forty-five seconds in which to look at Part Two.

[pause]

tone

My name's Rebecca Martin and I'm a pilot for Paradise Airlines, and I'd like to tell you about what I do in a typical day's work.

About an hour before the flight is due to leave I'll be in the crew room checking the flight plan and notices – information about the airports we'll be flying to. Today, there's a warning about birds in Athens. Swallows for example aren't such an issue, but today it's geese, which is another matter; you wouldn't want one of those going through your engine so we'll keep a look-out for them. Otherwise it looks as if we won't be running into anything complicated like storms or fog.

Today we'll be flying to Athens, then Rome, onto Paris and back to the UK. There'll be two pilots on board, so we can take a break but no stopover, fortunately. Some of the crew see these as one of the attractions of the job, especially in destinations like Athens, but I prefer my own bed. Luckily, I only have to do one or two long–haul flights per month which involve being away from home. I usually do the long–haul African and Asian routes and there we make sure there is a second fully qualified captain aboard – that amounts to a minimum six thousand flying hours between us. And it's not unheard of to have a first officer as an extra pair of hands on these trips – that's someone with fifteen hundred hours' flying experience.

I talk to my co-pilot about the pre-flight preparations. What he does is calculate the amount of fuel we're going to need which means working out the weight of the plane, plotting the route into the computer and allowing a bit extra for contingencies such as if we get diverted for one reason or another or have to circle an airport for half an hour waiting for permission to land, which happens on a regular basis.

Pilots definitely need a good head for figures to do all these calculations. I don't have a degree, which would be a pre-requisite these days, but I did pass exams in maths, physics and chemistry and I'd say all of us have a strong science background.

Even when I was a young child, I thought I might like to see the world one day, but these dreams were just a vague desire, and becoming a pilot wasn't exactly a burning passion for me, at that stage. But then I left school to train as an insurance broker and after a few years thought 'Do I really want to spend the next forty years doing this?' So then I got my private flying licence and one thing led to another and here I am: an airline pilot. It took me a while to get used to the expectations people have of you. We're thought of as superior beings by the rest of the cabin crew, and they sometimes even call us that, though I suspect they're not entirely serious. But you do need to develop something that's summed up in the phrase 'a sense of calm' – if you don't have that, people won't have confidence in you or respect you and that's a real problem for an airline pilot.

And of course you get to see a lot of the world. The highlight of any trip for me is a night flight if the sky is clear. It's magical. You can see stars galore above you and the lights of cities laid out below. My favourite destination is Mombasa in Kenya where I can sometimes fit in a coach trip, and last month I was lucky enough to go on safari, which I'd always wanted to do, although unfortunately it was the rainy season.

Friends outside work can struggle to understand why you aren't available on Friday or Saturday evenings. It really helps that the work of my partner, who's an air traffic controller, also involves antisocial hours. We don't have children, but one of my friends is a pilot who has three children, so she's having a hard time of it.

Anyway, coming back to today's flight, the next thing [*fade*]

[pause]

Now you will hear Part Two again.

tone

[The recording is repeated.]

[pause]

That is the end of Part Two.

Now turn to Part Three.

[pause]

PART 3

You will hear a radio interview with Olivia Glydon and Ron Partridge, who are hyperpolyglots, people who can speak many languages. For questions 16 to 20, choose the answer (A, B, C or D) which fits best according to what you hear.

You now have one minute in which to look at Part Three.

[pause]

tone

Interviewer:	With me today are two hyperpolyglots – that's people who can speak multiple languages. There's Olivia Glydon who at the age of twenty can already speak twenty-five languages. And Ron Partridge who can speak an incredible fifty languages and has written a book called 'Speaking in many tongues'. So Olivia, why the need to speak so many languages?
Olivia:	I think for me it's just that I'm into the way languages work. I just like them for their own sake really – using them as a communication tool is just a great by-product. In fact I've only ever had the opportunity to travel outside the United States once so all my communication is via Skype and email.
Ron:	Yes – and when you say I speak fifty languages that's not to say I'm fluent in all those languages – I have a working knowledge of them but I'm nowhere near the level of a native speaker. But I just love discovering more about the technical aspects of a language. Also the more you learn the easier it becomes to pick up additional languages. Now I'd only need a month or so to get to grips with the alphabet, pronunciation and grammar of any language.
Interviewer:	Would you say being a hyperpolyglot is something of a minority sport?
Olivia:	Well, in fact it was incredible to read Ron's book and find how typical my experience was of becoming a hyperpolyglot. I hadn't realised there were so many of us around.
Ron:	Yes it's nice to know there are other people who share your passion. And occasionally you'll find someone who's chosen the same obscure language to learn – so you can communicate via that. But when I was writing the book I discovered that hyperpolyglots have only been around since the nineteenth century, when people began to travel more. And the debate about whether the ability to learn multiple languages is an innate skill or whether it's learned started back then. Now we know that some people have a natural gift, though it certainly helps if you're bilingual or trilingual to begin with. That applied to me as my mother's Dutch.
Interviewer:	And how do people react to it? For me, with my very rusty French, it seems an almost superhuman feat.
Ron:	Incomprehension as to how we do it, coupled with awe, is a fairly typical reaction.
Olivia:	Yeah – some people can also be a bit suspicious – like there must be something weird about us or we've got suspect motives for wanting to learn dozens of languages. But generally people all over the world are really enthusiastic and willing to teach me Hindi, Arabic, Turkish, Kurdish, Dutch – or whatever. They get a kick out of it. That makes me feel good.
Ron:	Yes. For so long all the traffic has been in the opposite direction with English becoming so dominant, so I find it quite moving to discover that people are so proud of their native tongue.
Interviewer:	So Olivia do you spend all your free time on the Internet learning these languages?

Olivia:	Pretty much. Up to fifteen hours a day during college vacations. But it's not like I'm passively watching TV all day. I'm learning stuff all the time. Even when I'm watching trashy soap operas or chat shows – things I wouldn't be caught dead watching in English but they're cool in Hindi. I don't think I'm abnormal or obsessive. It's just I've found my niche. And I get to have online relationships with people around the world that share my interest.
Interviewer:	Right. And what about you, Ron? I understand you've a particular affection for some languages?
Ron:	That's right. There's a nearly extinct language spoken by the few surviving members of an aboriginal group in East Asia. It's not a language I can easily use to converse with other people. It's not that it lacks words for things like car and computer but they're irrelevant in my case. But when I'm walking up in the hills I find myself thinking in this language because it has this mystical quality. It's terrible that the world is losing so many of these ancient languages.
Interviewer:	Well that's absolutely fascinating. Really, thank you so much for coming in [*fade*]

[pause]

Now you will hear Part Three again.

tone

[The recording is repeated.]

[pause]

That is the end of Part Three.

Now turn to Part Four.

[pause]

PART 4

Part Four consists of two tasks. You will hear five short extracts in which people are talking about commuting. Look at Task One. For questions 21 to 25, choose from the list (A to H) what general concern each speaker has about commuting. Now look at Task Two. For questions 26 to 30, choose from the list (A to H) how each speaker feels now about their journey. While you listen you must complete both tasks.

You now have forty-five seconds in which to look at Part Four.

[pause]

tone

Speaker One When I tell people about my commute, I always get a similar version of the same comment: *oh, that sucks. That must be such a drag.* And at first I'd be like: *yeah.* But lately I've discovered the upside of commuting, so to speak. Sure, it's a two-hour round trip but now I look at it as my time to de-stress after a long day. I'm sure anyone would love to live nearer their office and not have to worry about the constant hikes in cost of gas but unfortunately my current situation isn't conducive to that. So why not see the bright side – right?

[pause]

Speaker Two The thought of commuting two hours a day almost made me turn down the job. And initially it was as bad as I'd expected but after six weeks I joined a car pool so I didn't have to drive every day and two weeks in and I'm already beginning to see my commute in a different light. It's the only chance I get to contemplate on the day ahead. I save money this way and also don't create any pollution so win-win all round. A perceived drawback has turned out quite differently, thankfully. I seriously don't know how people do it long term without cracking up. It'd be way too stressful for me driving all that way alone.

[pause]

Speaker Three   If I wasn't driving, I'd think nothing of a forty-five to fifty minute commute. I'd sit on the train or bus and chat to other commuters or read or play on the phone or whatever, or even just stare happily out of the window at the scenery. Instead of which, I'm battling the traffic. It's true that it currently only takes me thirty minutes to get to work in the morning and a bit longer to get home, so I suppose it could be worse, but I still find it takes a lot out of me physically. And it's expensive too – if I used public transport and didn't run a car, I'd save a fortune.

[pause]

Speaker Four   Some companies offer incentives to encourage alternative methods of transport instead of automobiles like offering interest-free loans for new bikes, because they're into being green. But my company isn't prepared to pay for bus passes, or invest in showers or changing facilities to make cycling a realistic option, so there's only a few of us who do it. The other thing that puts people off cycling is the so-called danger factor but in my thirty years of commuting by bike I've never had a crash. Freewheeling down the hill into town in the early morning with the sun rising behind the office blocks makes me realise what a great town I live in.

[pause]

Speaker Five   Commuting can be when people get some of their most sustained reading or thinking done. It should be like a kind of third place between work and home. I wouldn't mind that at all but my commute is just one interminable hassle. It's not as if anyone gets any useful work done standing on a packed and stuffy train. There's nothing to see because it's mostly going through tunnels and you can't even strike up a conversation with anyone because they're too moody or they'd rather stare blankly ahead or plug into their MP3. It would help a lot if my job allowed me to work from home a couple of days a week but that's not on the cards.

[pause]

Now you will hear Part Four again.

tone

[The recording is repeated.]

[pause]

That is the end of Part Four.

There will now be a pause of five minutes for you to copy your answers onto the separate answer sheet. Be sure to follow the numbering of all the questions. I shall remind you when there is one minute left, so that you are sure to finish in time.

[Teacher, pause the recording here for five minutes. Remind your students when they have one minute left.]

That is the end of the test. Please stop now. Your supervisor will now collect all the question papers and answer sheets.

Sample answer sheet: Reading and Use of English

CAMBRIDGE ENGLISH
Language Assessment
Part of the University of Cambridge

Do not write in this box

SAMPLE

Candidate Name
If not already printed, write name in CAPITALS and complete the Candidate No. grid (in pencil).

Candidate Signature

Examination Title

Centre

Supervisor:
If the candidate is ABSENT or has WITHDRAWN shade here ⊂⊃

Centre No.

Candidate No.

Examination Details

0	0	0	0
1	1	1	1
2	2	2	2
3	3	3	3
4	4	4	4
5	5	5	5
6	6	6	6
7	7	7	7
8	8	8	8
9	9	9	9

Candidate Answer Sheet 1

Instructions

Use a PENCIL (B or HB). Rub out any answer you wish to change using an eraser.

Part 1: Mark ONE letter for each question.

For example, if you think **B** is the right answer to the question, mark your answer sheet like this:

| 0 | A | B | C | D |

Parts 2, 3 and **4:** Write your answer clearly in CAPITAL LETTERS.

For Parts 2 and 3 write one letter in each box. For example:

| 0 | E X A M P L E |

Part 1

1	A	B	C	D
2	A	B	C	D
3	A	B	C	D
4	A	B	C	D
5	A	B	C	D
6	A	B	C	D
7	A	B	C	D
8	A	B	C	D

Part 2

Do not write below here

9		9 1 0 u
10		10 1 0 u
11		11 1 0 u
12		12 1 0 u
13		13 1 0 u
14		14 1 0 u
15		15 1 0 u
16		16 1 0 u

Continues over ➡

Part 3

Do not write below here

17		17 1 0 u
18		18 1 0 u
19		19 1 0 u
20		20 1 0 u
21		21 1 0 u
22		22 1 0 u
23		23 1 0 u
24		24 1 0 u

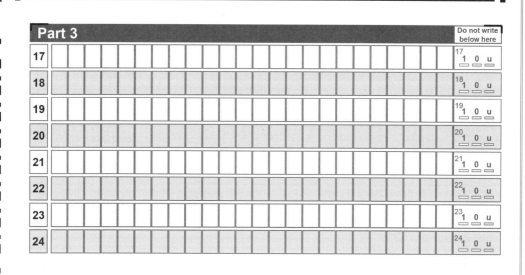

Part 4

Do not write below here

25		25 2 1 0 u
26		26 2 1 0 u
27		27 2 1 0 u
28		28 2 1 0 u
29		29 2 1 0 u
30		30 2 1 0 u

SAMPLE

denote Print Limited 0121 520 5100

Sample answer sheet: Reading and Use of English

CAMBRIDGE ENGLISH
Language Assessment
Part of the University of Cambridge

Do not write in this box

SAMPLE

Candidate Name
If not already printed, write name
in CAPITALS and complete the
Candidate No. grid (in pencil).

Candidate Signature

Examination Title

Centre

Supervisor:
If the candidate is ABSENT or has WITHDRAWN shade here ▭

Centre No.

Candidate No.

Examination Details

0	0	0	0
1	1	1	1
2	2	2	2
3	3	3	3
4	4	4	4
5	5	5	5
6	6	6	6
7	7	7	7
8	8	8	8
9	9	9	9

Candidate Answer Sheet 2

Instructions
Use a PENCIL (B or HB). Rub out any answer you wish to change using an eraser.

Parts 5, 6 and 7: Mark ONE letter for each question. For example, if you think **B** is the right answer to the question, mark your answer sheet like this:

Part 5

31	A	B	C	D
32	A	B	C	D
33	A	B	C	D
34	A	B	C	D
35	A	B	C	D
36	A	B	C	D

Part 6

37	A	B	C	D	E	F	G	H
38	A	B	C	D	E	F	G	H
39	A	B	C	D	E	F	G	H
40	A	B	C	D	E	F	G	H
41	A	B	C	D	E	F	G	H
42	A	B	C	D	E	F	G	H
43	A	B	C	D	E	F	G	H

Part 7

44	A	B	C	D	E	F
45	A	B	C	D	E	F
46	A	B	C	D	E	F
47	A	B	C	D	E	F
48	A	B	C	D	E	F
49	A	B	C	D	E	F
50	A	B	C	D	E	F
51	A	B	C	D	E	F
52	A	B	C	D	E	F
53	A	B	C	D	E	F

CPE R2

denote
Print Limited 0121 520 5100

DP755/191

© UCLES 2015 Photocopiable

162

CAMBRIDGE ENGLISH
Language Assessment
Part of the University of Cambridge

Do not write in this box

SAMPLE

Candidate Name
If not already printed, write name
in CAPITALS and complete the
Candidate No. grid (in pencil).

Candidate Signature ....

Examination Title

Centre

Centre No.

Candidate No.

Examination
Details

Supervisor:
If the candidate is ABSENT or has WITHDRAWN shade here ▭

Test version: A B C D E F J K L M N   Special arrangements: S H

Candidate Answer Sheet

Instructions

Use a PENCIL (B or HB).
Rub out any answer you wish to change using an eraser.

Parts 1, 3 and 4:
Mark ONE letter for each question.

For example, if you think **B** is the
right answer to the question, mark
your answer sheet like this:

Part 2:
Write your answer clearly in CAPITAL LETTERS.

Write one letter or number in each box.
If the answer has more than one word, leave one
box empty between words.

For example:

Turn this sheet over to start.

CPE L

DP756/192

© UCLES 2015   Photocopiable

SAMPLE

Part 1

1	A	B	C
2	A	B	C
3	A	B	C
4	A	B	C
5	A	B	C
6	A	B	C

Part 2 (Remember to write in CAPITAL LETTERS or numbers)

Do not write below here

7		7 1 0 u
8		8 1 0 u
9		9 1 0 u
10		10 1 0 u
11		11 1 0 u
12		12 1 0 u
13		13 1 0 u
14		14 1 0 u
15		15 1 0 u

Part 3

16	A	B	C	D
17	A	B	C	D
18	A	B	C	D
19	A	B	C	D
20	A	B	C	D

Part 4

21	A	B	C	D	E	F	G	H
22	A	B	C	D	E	F	G	H
23	A	B	C	D	E	F	G	H
24	A	B	C	D	E	F	G	H
25	A	B	C	D	E	F	G	H
26	A	B	C	D	E	F	G	H
27	A	B	C	D	E	F	G	H
28	A	B	C	D	E	F	G	H
29	A	B	C	D	E	F	G	H
30	A	B	C	D	E	F	G	H

denote Print Limited 0121 520 5100

Visual materials for the Speaking test

1B

1A

1C

2B

2A

2C

3B

3D

3A

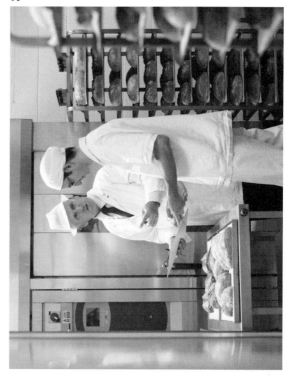

3C

4B

4A

TEST 1

What helps people to cooperate with others?

- personalities
- responsibilities
- objectives

TEST 2

How important is it to celebrate the special occasions in our lives?

- traditions
- relationships
- memories

TEST 3

Is it better to plan or to leave things to chance?

- pressure
- security
- opportunity

TEST 4

What are the advantages and disadvantages of parents telling their children what to do?

- safety
- learning
- responsibility

TEST 1

Prompt card 1b

What can be gained by learning in a group?

- different ages
- different skills
- different abilities

TEST 2

Prompt card 2b

How easy is it for young people to learn about important events in history?

- books
- films
- museums

TEST 3

Prompt card 3b

What part does chance play in success?

- sport
- business
- the arts

TEST 4

Prompt card 4b

What are the most important qualities needed to be a successful manager?

- personality
- experience
- communication skills